TAKING FLIGHT

TAKING FLIGHT

Making Your Center for Teaching and Learning Soar

Laura Cruz, Michele A. Parker,

Brian Smentkowski, & Marina Smitherman

Foreword by Cher Hendricks

STERLING, VIRGINIA

COPYRIGHT © 2020 BY STYLUS PUBLISHING, LLC.

Published by Stylus Publishing, LLC.
22883 Quicksilver Drive
Sterling, Virginia 20166-2019

Library of Congress Cataloging-in-Publication-Data
The CIP data for this title has been applied for.

13-digit ISBN: 978-1-64267-020-2 (cloth)
13-digit ISBN: 978-1-64267-021-9 (paperback)
13-digit ISBN: 978-1-64267-022-6 (library networkable e-edition)
13-digit ISBN: 978-1-64267-023-3 (consumer e-edition)

Printed in the United States of America

All first editions printed on acid free paper
that meets the American National Standards Institute
Z39-48 Standard.

Bulk Purchases
Quantity discounts are available for use in workshops and
for staff development.
Call 1-800-232-0223

First Edition, 2020

In 2016, participants at the Professional and Organizational Development (POD) Network's annual conference were invited by then-president Kevin Barry to write a thank-you card to someone who made a difference in their lives and careers. One of the most audible responses was "Just one?" And so it is with this book. The list is simply too long and our gratitude too great to fit in the space of a single page. We opt instead to thank all of those whose work has improved the academy and contributed so much to the generative culture of learning, leading, growing, and developing that defines our field. To all of those who have challenged and inspired us—and continue to do so, across academic generations and disciplines—thank you.

With special acknowledgments to the contributions of Cher Hendricks and Michele DiPietro, both of whom participated directly in Taking Flight before it became a book.

CONTENTS

My best moments in educational development happen in two places—on campus in the middle of an event where faculty are engaged in work that excites them and at conferences when educational developers come together to talk about their work. My best on-campus moments have only been possible because of what I've learned from my peers, most often at the Professional and Organization Development (POD) Network Conference that meets each fall. From my peers I've learned how to build things. Early in my career, I attended POD's Institute for New Faculty Developers with the goal of learning how to build a center for teaching and learning. What I started to discover then, and what I've continued to learn since, is that building a center requires more than building programs. We must also craft relationships and networks. We have to create strategic plans to guide our work and then develop an assessment process to see how we're doing. We have to build a communication strategy for a wide range of stakeholders. It's no small feat, and it can seem overwhelming to a new educational developer.

In truth, all this crafting, developing, and building can seem overwhelming to a more experienced educational developer, too. Institutional priorities shift. Sometimes this means educational developers are asked to do more or to take on different responsibilities. In some cases, particularly when resources are limited, we may find we have to justify our value. We may even be asked to do less. Whether building a new center or breathing new life into an existing one, the work is challenging, and it requires a broad range of skills.

One way to develop those skills is to take your time working through *Taking Flight*. This book was written by educational developers for educational developers, and it is based on research as well as the authors' experiences. These experiences include the good, the bad, and the ugly. They represent successes and failures, good days and bad, moments of inclusion and exclusion, and times when resources were abundant and scarce. The authors have considered their experiences, as well as what they've learned from their peers and from educational development literature, to provide you with the tools you need to develop your flight plan. This flight plan can help you get off the ground and soar, whether you are new to the field or experienced, operating as a center of one or responsible for leading a large team. As you work your way through this book, you'll learn how to take stock of where you are now, decide where you want to go, and determine whether you've reached your intended destination. You will learn strategies for building networks and communicating with different stakeholder groups. You will complete activities to determine institutional needs, set priorities, and lobby for a seat the table where big decisions are made.

The authors of this book came to faculty development in much the same way you probably did, from the faculty ranks and because of their interest in teaching and learning. It's likely that you've had little or no formal training in educational or faculty development and that, like the rest of us, you have learned on the fly. If you have built a center, or you are building one, or even if you are revitalizing an existing center, you may feel like you're building the plane while you're flying it. You may feel like you're already taking flight but without a clear flight plan. Know that you are in good company and that you have a strong peer network that is ready and willing to help you succeed.

Four members of that network are the authors of this book. The five of us delivered a Taking Flight workshop at the POD Network conference a few years back, and the idea for this book started to take shape as we debriefed after the workshop. Participants clearly needed more than a one-day session on how to start or revitalize a center for teaching and learning. It was evident that with our varied experiences, we had a lot to learn from each other. But we also realized we had much to offer, particularly if we combined our experiences. I have been grateful to cheer from the sidelines as Laura, Brian, Michele, and Marina committed to the task of writing this book. They have been able to weave together their experiences, evidence-based practices, and theory to provide a practical approach for building (or rebuilding) a center for teaching and learning. The result of their hard work is a book that will sit on your desk, not on your shelf. You will find yourself coming back to it over and over again as you engage in your educational development work. And once you take flight, that work—and what you learn from it—may even contribute to future editions of *Taking Flight*.

Cher Hendricks
Vice Provost, Academic Initiatives, University of Idaho

ACKNOWLEDGMENTS

Many thanks to Lindsay Martinez for the design of the Taking Flight logo.

INTRODUCTION

What Is Taking Flight?

In a nutshell, Taking Flight is a practical, hands-on, evidence-based and systematic approach to supporting educational developers (and related roles) in their efforts to start, revitalize, grow, and sustain a center for teaching or learning (or similar unit) on their respective college or university campuses.

The Taking Flight approach emphasizes elevating educational development to the level of the organization and how we can think intentionally about the roles we play in fostering teaching and learning communities at institutions with a wide range of missions and culture.

Where Did Taking Flight Come From?

Four educational developers walk into a bar. This may sound like the setup for a corny joke, but instead it served as the very real beginnings of the Taking Flight project. The authors happened to find themselves sitting together after a day of sessions at a national conference on educational development. A few of us knew each other, some better than others, but it was the first time all four of us sat down and talked. We determined that we did not seem to have much in common—at least not at first. One of us had recently switched institutions to start a new center for teaching and learning (CTL); another was leading a long-standing center that had recently had to undergo a significant revitalization; a third had founded her center over a decade ago, but felt it needed to find new directions; and a fourth had been consulting with international institutions on how to establish and sustain CTLs.

Educational developers are highly trained to practice empathy and search for common ground, so it is perhaps not surprising that we began to find connections and felt much less alone. As these things seem to happen at conferences, we started to get excited about the possibilities for pooling our hard-earned experiences into a single pot of cumulative wisdom. The fire of idealism burned ever brightly, and together we became committed to paying forward the lessons we had learned. Our voices got more animated; our hand gestures more dramatic; drawings were made on cocktail napkins; language was drafted. Somewhere around midnight in a medium-sized city in the American midwest, Taking Flight took flight. Since that time, we have spent several years honing the model by scouring the literature, editing our materials, hosting workshops, and, now, bringing what we have created to you in the form of this book. Cheers.

You Are Not Alone—Your Institution

Is your institution looking to found, revitalize, sustain, or reframe the work of its CTL (or similar unit)? Then you are not alone.

As a field, faculty development started in the 1950s. In the United States, the first generation of CTLs started popping up in the 1960s, with the primary mission of serving as a bridge between a growing body of research on teaching and learning, much of it coming out of psychology and education, and the faculty (Grant et al., 2009; Lewis, 1996; Ouellett, 2010). As the number of centers proliferated, so did the number of people working in the field, culminating in the creation of the Professional and Organizational Development (POD) Network, now the leading professional organization for educational developers in the United States (Ortquist-Ahrens, 2016). A similar pathway defines the historical trajectory of educational development in other countries, culminating in the creation of a number of national organizations, all of whom work together through the International Consortium for Educational Development (ICED; Lewis & Kristensen, 1997). Among other roles, these organizations serve as advocates for the value of educational development.

Along with a growing volume of research in teaching and learning transformation (the basis for evidence-based practice), this advocacy led to sustained expansion. By the 1980s, it had become commonplace for universities of all shapes, sizes, and missions to designate people, resources, and spaces to the pursuit of educational development (Murray, 2002). Today, it is estimated that there are over 2,000 CTLs (or similar units) in the United States alone. Over the years, individual CTLs have closed, scaled back, expanded, integrated, combined . . . you name it, all in response to changes in campus culture. Even beyond the walls of campus, we all work in a very dynamic sector of the economy—higher education is currently undergoing a period of the most rapid change it has experienced since (arguably) the eighteenth century. If there is one certainty, it is that the role of educational development, and the centers that shepherd its principle and practices, will continue to evolve (Gibbs, 2013; Land, 2001).

Speaking of evolution, let's take a minute to talk about nomenclature. In the United States, during the early years of the field, the most common term for what we do was called *faculty development*. This reflected our emphasis on the role of the teacher, as well as our focus on working with individuals (Sorcinelli, Austin, & Eddy, 2006). While we began primarily by doing one-on-one consultations, our role has significantly expanded since then, in terms of both scale and scope. In recognition of this expanding scope, leaders in the field have suggested that we change our name. In countries such as the United Kingdom and Australia, the preferred term that has emerged is *academic development* and in the United States, *educational development*. Both are umbrella terms for a myriad of practices including instructional, professional, personal, and organizational development, as well as work ranging from partnerships with faculty, programs, colleges, communities, and campuses (Leibowitz, 2014; Little, 2014). Regardless of what we do, whom we do it for, or what we call it, our core remains focused on fostering flourishing communities of teaching and learning (Felten, Kalish, Pingree, & Plank, 2007).

You Are Not Alone—Your Career

The shift toward the broader umbrella of educational development is indicative of a number of changes to the field, including our demographics. As the number of CTLs has expanded, so has the number of people who do educational development for a living, including, of course, you. Although our numbers are growing, you may still feel like you are by yourself. It is not uncommon for educational developers to be the only one (or one of a few) serving in such a role on their campus, a condition we refer to as being "organizationally lonely" in particular for "centers-of-one." Our organizational loneliness can be compounded by what scholars call our liminal state, meaning that we tend to operate somewhere between the level of course and whole campus and hold positions between the level of faculty member and senior administrator (Green & Little, 2013; Little & Green 2012).

Speaking of working between the levels of faculty and senior administrator, the majority of us who work in this field cut our teeth, so to speak, as faculty members before moving into educational development. If this description does not apply to you, there's no need to worry. The pathways into our profession have always been diverse and seem to be getting more so as we expand (McDonald & Stockley, 2008). For example, we are seeing a growing percentage of educational developers who are joining our ranks straight out of graduate school, a phenomenon that has led to our work often being cited as a vital part of the emerging alt-ac (which stands for alternative academic career) movement (Abbot & Gravett, 2017). There is also a small but growing percentage of us who come from other professions, including positions outside of academia. With or without a PhD, we represent a wide range of disciplinary backgrounds, with a slight preponderance for humanities and education (at least in the United States), but there are almost no disciplines that are not represented somewhere in our ranks (Green & Little, 2016). What you studied in graduate school (or taught as a faculty member or learned from experience in the workplace) is less important than what you choose to do with it.

It is not always easy to define who we are and what we do. Because of the diversity of pathways and professions into and within our profession, there is an emerging field of study that examines our collective identity and how we navigate and develop our individual roles over time (Manathunga, 2006). It is not uncommon for educational developers to have multiple identities, as we may continue to serve as faculty or hold other administrative posts simultaneously (Winter, 2009). In some ways, educational developers are jacks of all trades, as we usually work across multiple disciplines and are expected to have expertise in a wide range of teaching and learning topics, while we also seek to be recognized for our deep mastery of a specific field, for example, evidence-based practice in teaching and learning (Green & Little, 2017). As we continue to shift toward a focus on organizational development, more and more of us are including leader not just as a role, but also as part of our identity.

You Are Not Alone—Your Challenge

If you are reading this book, it is likely because you currently serve in or are about to be thrust into a position of leadership on your campus.

As an educational developer, you are probably familiar with the old chestnut that faculty claim to have been thrown into teaching without having had any previous preparation for doing so. Graduate programs, the story goes, train faculty to be researchers, not teachers. While we know that this is becoming less the case, especially with the continued rise of impressive graduate student development programs at many research universities, the story has served a constructive purpose as an impetus toward the creation of such programs, as well as others designed to fill this gap in professional development and pathways.

We are seeing a similar dynamic within our own field. Faculty are being asked to take on the role of educational developers without having any previous preparation for doing so. Their prior experience has trained them to be teachers and scholars, not staff or administrators. In the early years, CTLs primarily served as support units, the relevant research could be mastered relatively easily, and little additional training seemed necessary. That has certainly changed. The research on teaching, learning, professional development, and higher education has gone from a trickle to a flood, to the point that some now regard it as a separate academic discipline (Clegg, 2012), and we are being called on to not only master this burgeoning literature but also connect it effectively to institutional priorities (Haras, Taylor, Sorcinelli, & van Hoene, 2017). At our current trajectory, CTLs are shifting away from peer educator models and serving as change agents on our campuses (Diamond, 2005) a process one scholar has referred to as "coming in from the margins" (Schroeder, 2012). Many of us, even those of us who have been doing this work for a while, are getting a seat at the table for the first time, and we find ourselves doing so while facing very different challenges than our predecessors (Weimer, 2007). Our progress certainly is heady and exciting stuff, but it is perhaps unsurprising that researchers have recently looked at the prevalence of an imposter syndrome among us (Parkman, 2016; Rudenga & Gravett, 2019).

Let us assure you that you are not an imposter, but your ability to effect change will be enhanced by finding the right professional development opportunities to extend your knowledge base and refine your leadership skills and potential. Appreciating a vision and mission; developing strategic goals for your CTL; advocating at all levels of college structure for evidence-based practice; working effectively with staff, faculty, and/or upper administrators (maybe even rotating upper administrators); uncovering the logistics of achieving goals within their institution; building up and managing your reputation—all while finding a balance between all of your roles and responsibilities—every one of these is critical to your success. This lengthy list should be viewed not as a set of challenges, but as opportunities. Even the most experienced administrator cannot be effective without continually evaluating and developing their skills, adding to the depth of their experiences; and learning from others. With Taking Flight, we will provide you (and your colleagues) with multiple opportunities to sharpen your leadership saw.

You Are Not Alone—Regardless of Where You Are

With Taking Flight, we want to build a support and professional development structure for educational developers as leaders and administrators. This
is not a universal or monolithic process. Recently, scholars and practitioners have taken note that faculty go through developmental stages in their
careers, and that includes teaching (Bataille & Brown, 2006; Fugate & Amey,
2000; O'Meara, Terosky, & Neumann, 2008). We have responded to this by
developing targeted programs that meet the specific needs of faculty/instruc-
tors at their respective stages (Kalivoda, Sorrell, & Simpson, 1994; Zeig &
Baldwin, 2013). This has been especially evident, for example, in attention
being paid to midcareer faculty and the institutional attention that has been
paid to addressing the "stalled associate" or the "stuck professor" phenomenon (Corcoran & Clark, 1985; Grant-Vallone & Ensher, 2017). Turning
this lens back on ourselves, educational development researchers have started
to move past looking at how we enter into the field and are now beginning to examine our own glass ceilings, identify stages of career development,
and develop strategies for maintaining vitality over the long run (Bernhagen
& Gravett, 2017).

Organizations, too, go through life cycles; and we have organized *Taking
Flight* to follow the path of a CTL, starting from its origins as a glimmer in
someone's eye to its maturity as a thriving part of a campus community. These
stages are neither mutually exclusive nor exhaustive. It should be noted, too,
that this is intended to be an iterative loop (figure 1.1). Even if your center
has already been in existence for decades, you will still have opportunities to
build toward the next flight of your mission.

Stage 1: Building Your Nest

If you are fortunate enough to be in charge of starting a new center from the
ground up, then please let us extend our heartiest congratulations. At this
level, you are laying the groundwork for a long-range vision that will shape
both your center and your campus. It is a tremendous opportunity for positive impact, and also an increasingly rare one. As educational development
has continued to expand as a field, more institutions have embraced its value
and, consequently, there are fewer places that are untouched by the work that
we do.

Even if you are not the first to go there, it is likely that your task may
seem daunting at times. Never fear—the others who have gone before you
have left a trail of bread crumbs, that is, best practices for you to follow. This

Figure 1.1. Taking Flight CTL life-cycle model.

stage has been the focus of attention in the literature of both research and practice (D'Avanzo, 2009; Gray & Shadle, 2009), as well as any number of guides, workshops, and professional development opportunities. We also learn directly from each other; it is not uncommon for those charged with establishing new centers to visit any number of established centers and glean the wisdom of their staff, a form of pilgrimage that is viewed as a rite of passage into the field.

Stage 2: Learning to Fly

In the first stage, you've built the foundations for your new (or revitalized) center. Now it's time for the fledgling stage, where you strengthen your tool kit and put the people and resources in place to reach new heights. Although the first stage often involves considerable attention to education and advocacy for the work of the CTL, this second stage focuses on building your capacity.

In some respects, stage 2 is about identifying and implementing your portfolio of programs and initiatives. In the field of educational development, we have developed a standard menu of program offerings, for example, faculty learning communities, book groups, new faculty orientation, scholarship of teaching and learning, and graduate student development activities. The practice literature is replete with assessment, case studies, exemplars, and templates for implementing these successfully.[1]

With the rise of attention to organizational development, on the other hand, we are starting to see a divergence in practice, as CTLs are tasked with identifying educational development opportunities and initiatives that are tailored to the mission and culture of their respective institutions (Kelley, Cruz, & Fire, 2017). More than ever, it will take imagination on our part to adapt what we know from evidence-based practice and find ways to leverage what we know in the service of organizational change.

Stage 3: Soaring High

At the risk of belaboring our bird metaphor, the soaring high stage perhaps bears more similarity to the biology of birds than the others. When birds soar, it means they have reached their target altitude and they set their wings to maximize energy and efficiency, making small corrections as conditions change. Similarly, CTLs in this third stage have reached the desired capacity levels and much of their work focuses on maintaining their lofty position. This does not mean stagnation; rather, it is about smaller corrections, micro-adaptions, versus radical change (to use the current lingo, this is also called continuous improvement or improvement science).

Soaring high also involves finding the right balance to maintain your altitude. CTLs are notorious for being targets of mission creep, that is, more and more responsibilities piling up on your plate. It can be challenging to determine what to say yes to and what to say no to, what to maintain and what to scrap; in other words, what you need to stay aloft and what might bring you down to earth (Siering, Tapp, Lohe, & Logan, 2015). This can also be about refining your alignment with institutional goals and priorities. For these reasons, stage 3 is often a time of reflection and taking stock: looking back on what you have accomplished, sharing what you've learned with others, and laying the groundwork for where you might go in the future.

Stage 4: Returning Home

Just as the swallows return to Capistrano each year, we should find ways to periodically renew our focus on the evolving mission to enhance teaching and learning communities on our respective campuses. The renewal process can be painful. Sometimes it may mean getting rid of, or radically altering, long-standing and beloved programs. Sometimes it may mean repurposing staff or moving budgets. Sometimes it can mean discarding outmoded thinking and becoming connected to new movements, initiatives, evidence, or campus leadership.

While this can be seen as a disruptive stage, these changes also serve a constructive purpose, laying the groundwork for what's coming next for you and your CTL. Rather than seeing this as a reactive stage, you can use this as an opportunity to be proactive and look at what's coming down the road, find innovative solutions to persistent challenges, and set the stage for what lies ahead. To write the next chapter of the story takes vision as well as the ability to impart knowledge and enthusiasm and inspire others to follow as you get ready to build your new nest.

You Are Not Alone: We Are Here for You

You are not alone in facing these challenges or stages. Every member of the Taking Flight team has had the experience of building the skills, perspectives, and resources needed to lead a CTL through multiple stages of development. Along the way, we've laughed, cried, raged, cheered, despaired, and celebrated, as will you. Our team is committed to being by your side, serving as your print and virtual coaches, with a program that we've intentionally built from a place of evidence and empathy.

The Taking Flight approach reflects the values of the field of educational development (e.g., collegiality, inclusion, diversity, advocacy, distributed leadership, innovation, evidence-based practice, respect), and we try to model those practices in how we have designed and delivered the contents of this book. In addition, we have developed five principles, specific to the Taking Flight process, to guide our work (and yours):

1. Taking Flight is *practical*. This volume is not intended to be something you will curl up with in bed at night and get lost in reading, nor should you find it collecting dust on your library shelf. It contains tools, guides, resources, worksheets, and examples that you can use right now and in the future.

2. Taking Flight is *syncretic*. We bring together a wealth of evidence-based organizational strategies used in other contexts and integrate these into the specific context of educational development for higher education. We've read through all this stuff so you don't have to.

3. Taking Flight is *sustainable*. Drawing deeply from systems thinking, our approach emphasizes change over time and encourages thinking that transcends the immediate and extends to the long run. We're all in this for the long haul.

4. Taking Flight is *collaborative*. Our process looks to connect you with the experiences of others who are facing similar challenges and opportunities. You are not alone in wanting your center to flourish.

5. Taking Flight is *developmental*. Our resources are carefully selected to represent a wide range of experiences and expertise in the field. The volume is structured to meet you where you are and allow you to create plans that are custom tailored to meet your needs across a variety of stages of growth. As you complete each stage, we invite you to return to the Taking Flight tool kit.

How to Take Flight

First and foremost, you are encouraged to use this book however it may be useful to you.

That being said, we had envision that some readers may choose to follow the developmental cycle, returning to the text when they reach the milestones along the way. This would involve an essentially linear progression through the book's contents. In this sense, the book functions as a comprehensive guide.

Another type of reader may choose a "surgical strike," dipping into those resources or elements as they are needed to meet the professional development of the person or the organization. This reader may choose to copy certain pages or sheets and share them with others. In this sense, the book functions as a reference text. You will find a treasure trove of references and further reading at the end of the book.

Still another type of reader may view these resources as a form of preparation or professional development curriculum, leading toward a potential leadership role. We wish to encourage you in your aspirations.

Regardless of how or why you have chosen to take flight, we are grateful to have you with us and look forward to seeing you soar.

Note

1. Rather than bog down our prose with a long list of citations for these programs, we encourage everyone (if they do not already do so) to stay connected to the major journals in the field, such as *To Improve the Academy* (TIA), *the International Journal for Academic Development* (IJAD), and the *Journal of Faculty Development*, as well as to journals in related fields, such as the scholarship of teaching and learning (SoTL), engagement/service-learning, and higher education.

2

ESTABLISHING A BASELINE

Where Are You Now?

I learned to look more upon the bright side of my condition, and less upon the dark side, and to consider what I enjoyed, rather than what I wanted: and this gave me sometimes such secret comforts, that I cannot express them . . . All our discontents about what we want appeared to me to spring from the want of thankfulness for what we have.

—Daniel Defoe (1719), *The Life and Adventures of Robinson Crusoe*

In Daniel Defoe's (1719) well-known novel *Robinson Crusoe*, the titular British sailor finds himself shipwrecked on a desert island. At first, he is despondent over the apparent hopelessness of his condition. As time goes by, however, he inventories the resources available to him on the island and finds that the exercise changes his perspective, and not because he has an abundance of resources at his disposal. Rather, as the quote that opens this chapter implies, there is something in the act of taking stock that can have profound psychological effects. While you are not stranded on a desert island, you may find yourself in a new place where the environment is unfamiliar. Like Crusoe, you may find it helpful, even encouraging, to begin your adventures by exploring the people, places, and resources that characterize your new terrain.

This chapter presents you with the opportunity to explore specific ideas about *where you are now*. As a team we have extensive and varied experience with CTLs. Accordingly, we share a few approaches and tips we find helpful in establishing a baseline in a new or revitalized center. You may use any of these exercises or a combination of them to establish a baseline for the CTL whether it is new or at another stage on the continuum.

Step 1: Just the Facts

A first step in exploring your baseline is to read through formal documents, such as institutional organizational charts and strategic plans, as well as peruse the key sources of institutional data, especially those metrics that are most relevant to teaching and learning. Some suggested internal data sources to be acquainted with are student success metrics (including DWF rates which indicate the grades of students who do not successfully complete the course), grade distributions, student exit interviews and surveys, accessible data from student evaluations of instruction, and enrollment and demographic trends (usually accessible through the university fact book). In the United States, your institution may also subscribe to sources of national-level data, including instruments such as the National Survey of Student Engagement (NSSE), the Collaborative on Academic Careers in Higher Education (COACHE) survey, and the EDUCAUSE Center for Analysis and Research (ECAR) survey (student and faculty versions available). This is an especially crucial step for educational developers who are new to their campus, but even those who have served in other roles at an institution may wish to refresh or revise their knowledge of the people and offices of their campus in light of their new role (McCaffery, 2018).

Step 2: Listening

While formal documents can give you one perspective on how a campus operates, they do not give you the full picture. One of the primary pillars of educational development work is building relationships, and so you can often gain different perspectives by talking to as many people as possible and gleaning insights into how they work, what they value, and where they are headed. Often the most effective means for understanding the culture of an institution is accomplished informally through discreet observation, direct interaction, and personal conversations. While these sound like casual activities, they can be intentionally cultivated. You can set goals for the number of new people to reach out to, for example, or establish a set of questions to generate a list of contacts.

Taking Flight Tip: *Lunch With [Insert Your Name Here] Series*

One director (newly hired at a medium-sized regional comprehensive university) planned a weekly lunch series in which she had a friendly lunch with a different campus stakeholder each week and ended the meal by asking for names of people (the best teacher you know, the person people listen to when it comes to teaching, and someone who would simply be good to know). In turn, a similar invitation would be extended to these people in future weeks.

To further your thoughts about establishing a CTL baseline, imagine a scenario in which the associate director of the CTL at your campus contacts you for an urgent meeting. You schedule the meeting after your existing commitment. Upon arrival at the CTL, after exchanging pleasantries, the associate director asks, "Do you know why you are here?" You convey uncertainty, and the associate director explains they are moving into the director position and are seeking to fill the role being vacated. With gentle probing, you learn another faculty member, from your college, declined the opportunity already. Given your expertise you were recommended as a candidate, which is the reason for the meeting.

You ask the associate director about strengths, opportunities, and aspirations for the CTL. From the conversation you learn that upper level administration wants educational development programming to address diversity initiatives and wants to increase the participation rates of faculty from diverse backgrounds. While engaging in the conversation you are informally gathering information to *establish a baseline*. Essentially, you want to gather as much information as you can about internal and external factors that may influence the success of the CTL.

In wondering about the climate and procedures of the CTL, you ask the associate director to describe the CTL office culture and written as well as unwritten expectations. In discussing the specifics of the position, you learn that, among other tasks, the associate director is responsible for evaluating programming and annual reporting. During the next several days, you informally ask other people about the CTL while reflecting on the responses of the new director about strengths, weaknesses, opportunities, and threats. A few days later, excitedly, you accept the associate director position.

Upon assuming the position, you are asked to compose a one-page document of the CTL's highlights from the previous academic year to share with the newly hired provost for informational purposes. Because you are acclimating to this new role in the CTL, this is an opportunity to learn and apply the information with a fast approaching deadline. To establish a summary of what occurred prior, you rely on information from the CTL website. The evaluations (slips of paper) from weekly programming are shared with you. Quickly, you realize additional information is needed to formally capture the baseline.

Ask Yourself:
What other kinds of information would be helpful for you to know? To gather?

A simple mantra for educational developers is "Listen, learn, and lead" (Cohen, 2010). Listening to individuals is an integral part of how we do consultations, but it can also serve us well in listening to our institutions. There are many ways to listen, but here are a few that others have tried successfully:

- *Listening Booths*: These are private or semiprivate spaces where people (faculty, staff, students, or administrators) can record their thoughts, often implemented on a pop-up basis at events or in high-traffic areas.
- *Listening Tours*: These are similar to mobile focus groups, where you travel to various offices or buildings to meet with stakeholder groups, asking open-ended questions about the culture of teaching and learning on campus.
- Classroom Observations: Whether formal (e.g., with a small group diagnostic) or informal, watching how faculty teach (and how students respond to teaching) is your most direct source of information about campus norms.

For those of you without a background in ethnographic research, some aspects of this approach may seem a bit unstructured or undirected. As a counterexample, anthropologist Lauren Herckis (2018) recently spent time observing faculty across their typical workdays (e.g., in their offices, classrooms, and conference rooms and she was able to overturn a number of common assumptions about the sources of faculty resistance to teaching transformation. It should be noted that listening is only part of the equation; you will now have to consider how you will build an effective response to the insights you have gathered.

Step 3: Taking Stock

The next step involves moving from passive to active strategies for taking stock of your current campus climate.

Option 1: Strengths, Weaknesses, Opportunities, and Threats

Robinson Crusoe kept a running inventory of his goods by writing them down in lists. You may wish to use a more systematic approach. There are multiple ways to determine baseline information for your CTL. Strengths, weaknesses, opportunities, and threats (SWOT) analysis is one of the most well-known and commonly used tools for taking stock (Goetsch & Davis, 2014; Hax & Majluf, 1996; Osita, Idoko, & Justina, 2014; Rowley, 1997).

Using the SWOT framework, you can leverage the strengths and opportunities and identify ways to address potential or real weaknesses and threats. For example, if the honors college and writing center at your institution are CTL partners, how might the staff collaborate on educational development initiatives for the betterment of students?

To help establish a baseline, See Worksheet 2.1 and Figure 2.1 for two SWOT exercises that extend beyond the four categories typically used in work sessions. To begin, let's consider SWOT in relation to internal and external factors. Internal factors may involve "structure, systems and procedures, climate, physical, financial, and human resources" (Kock et al., 2004 as cited in Rabee, 2014, p. 259). Structure may pertain to the reporting structure of the center or it may pertain to how various units fit within the structure of the CTL. Meanwhile external factors may be "economic, competitive, social, political, legal and technological" (Kock et al., 2004 as cited in Rabee, 2014, p. 259). For example, consider a CTL that has new student-centered classrooms outfitted with the most recent technology, and imagine that the administration at your institution wants to adopt the same technology even though the resources (e.g., staff and financial) to support this change are unavailable. While this challenge is clearly dependent on the state of technology, it is also related to economic factors (what can the institution afford to do?) and competitive forces (what is driving the demand?).

To take stock of where you (and your CTL) are now, so that you can take flight later, we encourage you to examine each category in SWOT *as well as* internal and external factors, as depicted in worksheet 2.1. You can complete this exercise individually or use this as a worksheet that stakeholders can complete before discussing. Instead of using this as a handout, the activity can be conducted on flip charts or a white board with stakeholders organized in small groups that reconvene as a larger group. Regardless of how this exercise is implemented, internal and external factors can be captured in bullet points or truncated notes that can be converted into prose afterward. As you think about this within your CTL and context, remember strengths can come from within (internal) and from without (external). Meanwhile, weaknesses, opportunities, and threats can stem from within or can be precipitated by externalities.

The next activity focuses on (a) combinations of strengths and opportunities and (b) coupling strengths and threats (Verboncu & Condurache, 2016). According to Verboncu and Condurache (2016) using this methodology significantly improves the resulting information whether you are starting a new center or revitalizing an existing one. Let's say you identify three strengths or strong points, three weaknesses or weak points, and on. Next, think about how this information can be combined to provide a fuller picture for the CTL. Consider these possible combinations:

WORKSHEET 2.1
SWOT Analysis (With Internal and External Emphasis)

Strengths

These attributes and resources can support a successful outcome.

Internal Strengths	External Strengths

Weaknesses

These attributes or resources may hinder a successful outcome.

Internal Weaknesses	External Weaknesses

Opportunities

There are likely an abundance of opportunities and the key is being realistic.

Internal Opportunities	External Opportunities

Threats

Identifying potential threats provides a realistic mechanism for gauging adversity and means that they can be proactively addressed.

Internal Threats	External Threats

- Strengths and opportunities (SO strategies)
- Strengths and threats (ST)
- Weaknesses and opportunities (WO)
- Weaknesses and threats (WT strategies)

Once you identify the top three strengths, weaknesses, and so forth, it is easier to consider how combining these details may help a center take flight. For instance, by combining a strength and an opportunity you may realize an SO strategy that you can use to strengthen the CTL and desired outcomes. Likewise, thinking of a weakness (e.g., a CTL that is overscheduled) and an opportunity (e.g., increasing student enrollment) in tandem may help you identify ways to move the CTL forward. For example, given this WO, perhaps you and the provost have a conversation about additional staffing to help meet the needs of faculty given the increase in enrollment that has already occurred and is projected to continue into the following academic year. These examples show how combinations of strengths, weaknesses, opportunities, and threats can be considered together to help identify the starting point for leveraging this information to advance the mission of your CTL.

Option 2: Strengths, Opportunities, Aspirations, and Results

Another strategy for establishing a baseline is the strengths, opportunities, aspirations, and results (SOAR) technique. Although this approach is less

Figure 2.1. What SWOT may look like in a specific educational development context.

	Strengths, strong points (S) 1. 2. 3.	Weaknesses, weak point (W) 1. 2. 3.
Opportunities (O) 1. 2. 3.	SO Strategies 1. 2. 3.	WO Strategies 1. 2. 3.
Threats, constraints (T) 1. 2. 3.	ST Strategies 1. 2. 3.	WT Strategies 1. 2. 3.

Source: Verboncu & Condurache, 2016.

Figure 2.2. Example of completed SWOT matrix with combinations.

	Strengths, strong points (S) 1. Leadership support 2. Faculty champions 3. The CTL has a physical space	**Weaknesses, weak points (W)** 1. More staff needed 2. Budget could be bigger 3. There are more large (100+ students) classes than before
Opportunities (O) 1. Partner with the Office of Applied Learning 2. The Office of e-Learning is being reorganized 3. Leadership wants more online courses	**SO Strategies** 1. Leadership support and partnering with the Office of Applied Learning 2. Faculty may champion the reorganization of the Office of e-Learning to align with the CTL 3. The CTL has a physical space that can be used to work with faculty since leadership wants more online courses	**WO Strategies** 1. More staff needed and partner with the Office of Applied Learning 2. Budget could be bigger and the Office of e-Learning is being reorganized 3. There are more large classes than before and leadership wants more online courses
Threats, constraints (T) 1. Changes in leadership 2. Competing faculty needs 3. CTL event calendar is full	**ST Strategies** 1. Leadership support may not be stable given changes in leadership. 2. Faculty champions may help with competing faculty needs 3. The CTL has a physical space and CTL event calendar is full. How can we address this?	**WT Strategies** 1. More staff needed and there are changes in leadership 2. Budget could be bigger in order to address competing faculty needs 3. There are more large (100+ students) classes than before and CTL event calendar is full. Do we incorporate strategies for dealing with large classes into the existing programming?

Source: Verboncu & Condurache, 2016.

well known than SWOT, it is one of our favorites. Because it is based on appreciative inquiry, it can resonate well with the values of educational development.

Relevant definitions for the SOAR method follow are as follows:

- *Strengths:* What an organization is doing really well, including its assets, capabilities, and greatest accomplishments.
- *Opportunities:* External circumstances that could improve profits, unmet customer needs, threats, or weakness reframed into possibilities.
- *Aspirations:* What the organization can be; what the organization desires to be known for.
- *Results:* "The tangible, measurable items that will indicate when the goals and aspirations have been achieved" (ASQ Service Quality Division, 2016, para. 6).

This strengths-based strategy is a different approach to establishing your baseline, one that can serve as the foundation of your strategic plan (see Figure 5.1). In an established CTL, this approach can help us answer the following questions: What are we doing well? What skills can be improved? What is most compelling to stakeholders? In a new CTL, this approach can help us answer the following questions: What do we do well as a university? What skills can be improved? What is most compelling to stakeholders?

Figure 2.3. SOAR 5-I strategic planning approach.

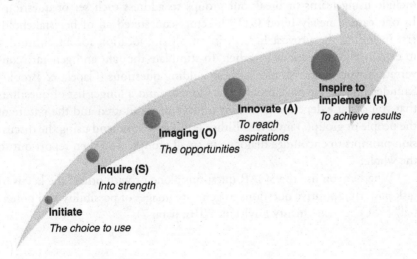

Inspire to implement (R)
To achieve results

Innovate (A)
To reach aspirations

Imaging (O)
The opportunities

Inquire (S)
Into strength

Initiate
The choice to use

Source: Capela & Brooks-Saunders (n.d.).

The activity for conducting your SOAR session can occur in one sitting or during a longer period of time. The choice depends on the purpose (e.g., annual goals versus five-year strategic plan) and other contextual factors (e.g., availability of stakeholders).

Ask Yourself:

- What is going well for you or your organization/CTL?
- Why do you care about the future of your organization/CTL?
- What can we build on?
- What are our greatest strengths?
- What are your stakeholders asking for?
- What are our best opportunities?
- What do we care deeply about?
- How do we know we are succeeding?
- What is our preferred future?
- What are the measurable results that will tell us we've achieved that vision of the future? (ASQ Service Quality Division, 2016, para. 3, 7).

Ideally stakeholders will be involved in the SOAR process. This may include using teams or break-out groups to address each set of questions. In one case, a newly hired CTL director sequestered all of her stakeholders, including the provost herself, in an off-site location for an entire day to explore these questions together. To stimulate thought and generate conversation, you may wish to use these guiding questions (Capela & Brooks-Saunders, n.d.). We have provided a short list and a longer list of questions that you can use depending on how much time is allotted and the nature of the people or group(s) involved. Either way, we recommend using the discussion prompts to encourage dialogue in small groups, who then report out to the whole.

Whether you use the SOAR questions alone or with others the key is to "ask powerful, positive questions to generate images of possibility and potential" (ASQ Service Quality Division, 2016, para. 7).

WORKSHEET 2.2
SOAR Questions

Strengths: What can you build on?

- What are we most proud of as an institution or CTL? How does that reflect our greatest strength?
- What makes us unique? What can we be best at in our world?
- What is our proudest achievement in the last year or two?
- How do we use our strengths to get results?
- How do our strengths fit with the realities of the marketplace?
- What do we do or provide that is world class for our students, our institution, and other potential stakeholders?

Opportunities: What are you/your stakeholders asking for?

- How do we make sense of opportunities provided by the external forces and trends?
- What are the top three opportunities on which we should focus our efforts?
- How can you best meet our needs (stakeholders, including students, employees, and the community)?
- How can you reframe challenges to be seen as existing opportunities?
- What new skills do we need to move forward?

Aspirations: What do you care deeply about?

- When we explore our values and aspirations, what are we deeply passionate about?
- Reflecting on strengths and opportunities conversations, who are we, who should we become, and where do we go in the future?
- What are your most compelling aspirations?
- What strategic initiatives (e.g., projects, programs, processes) would support your aspirations?

Results: How do we know you are succeeding?

- Considering our strengths, opportunities, and aspirations, what meaningful measures would indicate that we are on track to achieving your goals?
- What are three to five indicators that would create a scorecard that addresses a triple bottom line of profit, people, and planet?
- What resources are needed to implement vital projects?
- What are the best rewards to support those who achieve our goals?

Step 4: Mapping Your Terrain

Option 1: Environmental Scan

Robinson Crusoe may have been stranded on an isolated island, but you operate in the context of multiple environments. The internal part of SWOT or SOAR focuses on your institution, but an environmental scan process is usually focused on identifying and analyzing external threats and opportunities. A conventional environmental scan looks at four levels: immediate (e.g., your university); the industry (e.g., higher education); the field (e.g., educational development); and the macroenvironment, which includes large-scale social, political, and economic factors (Narayanan & Fahey, 2001). It is called a scan because it is by necessity a broad view, taken from your particular vantage point. Just as a shipwrecked sailor scans the horizon, you scan your environment to gather information on current conditions, to monitor trends and patterns, and to be prepared for what dangers or opportunities lie ahead.

Unlike these other planning tools, an environmental scan is not usually created through an open, collaborative process. Rather, it is essentially a research project in which you peruse the information available, including academic works social media, websites, and other nonacademic sources, and synthesize the most relevant information. Sources of higher education news, such as *Inside Higher Ed* or *The Chronicle of Higher Education*, can often be productive places to start. The information you gather serves, in turn, as the basis for further conversations with others. And it is really for these others that the scan is conducted, so be mindful of your audience when preparing the final product. Although you will likely wade through an ocean of sources, the most effective environmental scans are short and readable, conveyed perhaps in the form of bullet points or infographic elements (Worksheet 2.3). Fortunately, this form of environmental scanning is a familiar process for most institutions of higher education (Friedel & Rosenberg, 1993; Kezar, 2001; Meixell, 1990), which should benefit you in presenting your work to senior administrators.

WORKSHEET 2.3
CTL Environmental Scanning Template

Context	Current Conditions	Emerging Trends and Patterns	Future Challenges and Opportunities
Institution			
Higher Education			
Educational Development			
State/Region			
World			

Option 2: Political, Economic, Social, Technological, Environmental, and Legal Analysis

Tools such as SWOT or SOAR are frequently accompanied by analyses that focus on not only the work that you do but also the broader context in which you operate (Narayanan & Fahey, 2001). If you'd prefer a more collaborative tool for exploring the external forces that affect your opportunities and threats, you may wish to consider a political, economic, social, technological, environmental, and legal (PESTEL) analysis. It should be noted that the framework is flexible, and others have incorporated additional balloons such as aesthetic, intercultural, demographic, and historical factors (Schmieder-Ramirez & Mallette, 2015). In other words, you can create your own personal PESTEL as you see fit (even if the acronym doesn't come out quite as snappy). While the purpose of PESTEL overlaps with SWOT and SOAR, one of its additional benefits is that it provides an inherently visual representation, a map of sources, which reflects the interdependent nature of educational development work (R. Collins, 2010).

One of the biggest challenges in PESTEL analysis is not filling in the spaces, but rather having too many boxes. An argument can be made that almost any external factor has some kind of influence on the work of teaching and learning; the secret to success is to focus on identifying the most relevant factors in each sector. For this reason, experienced PESTEL facilitators often emphasize the evidence base for claims of relevance, which can serve to moderate the influence of personal opinions or passions.

Now that you've studied, listened, watched, explored, and mapped, you are ready to serve as the ambassador between your institution and the field of educational development. You are our representative on your campus. While this may appear to be a secondary concern (at least at the beginning), Todd Zakrajsek (2010) argued that understanding our own field is perhaps the most essential skill we can cultivate, at least in part because this allows us to bring to bear the wisdom of thousands of our colleagues on the conditions present on your campus. Although he emphasized engagement in the published literature, conferences, conversations with colleagues, and a multitude of ancillary resources, his premise extends into our own field of play, so to speak: your own little island. Just as Robinson Crusoe faced both expected and unexpected constraints and opportunities, we too need to mind our own backyard and scan the horizon for what lies ahead. To put it another way, a baseline process can help us to know our lane(s) and how to be most effective within them, and with whom to collaborate when we can not solve issues alone. By reading *Taking Flight*, you've pitched your tent, so to speak, so now let's turn toward the next steps with which you can take what you have and turn it into what you want.

Figure 2.4. PESTEL analysis for CTLs.

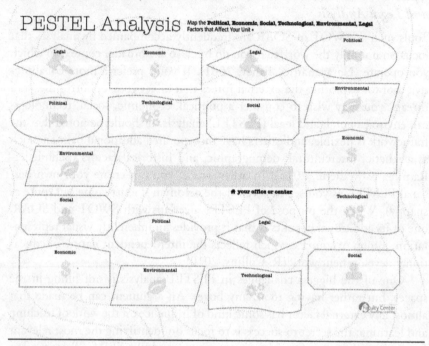

Source: Drake, Bowdon, & Saitta (2012).

3

NEEDS ASSESSMENT

What Do They Need?

The concept of need has an interesting history in pop culture, evoked by everyone from Aristotle to Marx to Mick Jagger. Etymologically speaking, the word comes from middle English and connotes lack or lacking. It may be helpful, then, to delineate not just what a need is, but what it lacks. According to the precepts of logic, an argument can be necessary and/or sufficient; to be necessary (or needed) means that the condition is required in order for the desired outcome to occur, but it may not be sufficient in and of itself to produce that outcome. The necessary precedes the sufficient cause, and it can come either before or after what we want, if the Rolling Stones are to be believed. That is, our wants are expressions of our desired outcomes, which we can only hope might come to pass. And Marx hoped that it would come to pass that our wants and needs would, perhaps one day (when scarcity no longer exists), be the same. The challenge of doing your needs assessment is that people reverse the necessary and sufficient, confuse needs and wants, and struggle to see the big picture beyond their own personal horizons. What you will find, though, is that if you try sometimes, especially with a thoughtful needs assessment process, you may get your stakeholders what they need *and* what they want.

Taking Flight Scenario

Consider a scenario in which you are the director or staff member of a CTL faced with lots of different kinds of data (at least some of which seems contradictory) and with the challenge of developing programming that responds to these data.

- Based on these data, what do you think the campus wants?
- Based on these data, what do you think the campus needs?
- What are the limitations of these sources of data or information?
- What other kinds of data or information would be helpful to have?

The Data

Imagine the following scenarios involving formal and informal data collection and information gathering:

- Working with individual faculty members—through one-on-one consultations and class observations—you have heard numerous faculty express frustration about their perception that student engagement is at an all-time low.
- In a recent speech announcing the university's new strategic plan, the president explained that a strong priority will be placed on student retention over the next five years.
- While serving on a campus-wide committee for learning technologies, you helped to design a faculty survey that seeks to understand how faculty experience the campus's learning management system (LMS; e.g., Blackboard, Canvas). The results of the survey suggest that faculty are unhappy with the LMS; they complained about a lack of basic functionality, but in the committee's discussions, it becomes clear that the functionality faculty members desire is already in place in the current LMS.
- During new faculty orientation, you led several workshops on designing collaborative, learning-centered assignments. Those new faculty who have never taught before expressed a strong desire to use such assignments, but they also indicated they would likely wait until their third or fourth semester of teaching, because they were new to the university and were feeling uncertain about their basic ability to convey information. In the follow-up evaluation, 92% of respondents expressed strong interest in learning about more engaging, interactive learning methods.
- The provost recently sent a memo to all deans and department/program heads indicating that she expects to see a significant increase in online course and program offerings over the next 12–18 months; she explained that she saw this as a way to build revenue and reputation. In response, the faculty senate prepared an open letter to the faculty at large, expressing their resistance to this initiative, in part because "it is impossible to achieve online the level of student/faculty interaction, student engagement, and deep learning that are crucial to the kind of education this university provides for students."
- At the end of the previous semester, your CTL staff members made a list of patterns they'd begun to see in the feedback from midsemester student focus groups. Among other things, students in multiple classes, across multiple departments, suggested that their instructors should "put all the information that will be tested on PowerPoint slides" and "post the slides to the LMS before class." Students also routinely said they wanted "more real-world examples" to supplement their learning (Chrystall & Lohe, 2015).

The Needs Assessment Process

Can you use the aforementioned data or information collected while establishing a baseline to help craft a needs assessment? Absolutely, but you may be looking for more. Conducting a needs assessment, which can be formal or informal, is a systematic means of gathering helpful information. With input from multiple stakeholder groups you can explore and discuss options for conducting formal and informal needs assessments on your campus. The basic premise of a needs assessment is simply asking faculty, students, and administrators to articulate their needs, but the entire process usually takes four steps: planning, doing, studying (the results), and acting upon what you find (see Figure 3.1).

One of the central tenets, or "Rs," of faculty development is being responsive (M. C. Wright, Lohe, Pinder-Grover, & Ortquist-Ahrins, 2018) and the needs assessment process is a means for you to respond strategically. As one associate provost puts it, "Needs assessments can help you learn about what different stakeholders on your campus need or want from their CTL" (Hendricks, 2015, para. 2). Accordingly, a needs assessment can help

Figure 3.1. The needs assessment process.

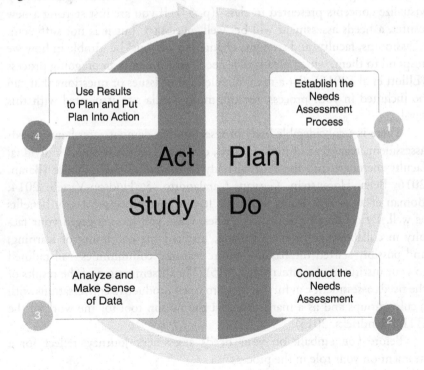

Source: Hendricks (2015).

you identify what is most important to different stakeholders (e.g., faculty [including across ranks and disciplines], administrators, staff, and campus leaders). For example, in a changing institutional context, Boman, Yeo, and Matus (2013) used a needs assessment to "gather information to guide the redevelopment of the institution's support program for new faculty" (p. 13). Via an online survey, "faculty were asked about support and resources they perceived themselves as needing during the first year of their full-time appointment and what gaps were present in their professional development" (p. 13). In contrast, Naliaka Mukhale (2017) used semistructured interviews to identify the professional development needs of lecturers. Similarly, Pastore (2013) used semistructured interviews to examine the needs of midcareer faculty. Administrators, instructional trainers, and staff in online learning programs are sources of information and support. Elliott, Rhoades, Jackson, and Mandernach (2015) highlight the need to work closely with these groups to determine the focus and format of faculty development programming.

Several researchers have noted ways in which students can be used to determine faculty development needs (Baran, 2016). The assessment process detailed entailed weekly meetings, classroom observations, social media feedback, and student questionnaires. Interestingly, the questionnaires revealed insights such as "students wanted classroom technologies to help visualize concepts presented in class" (p. 57). If you are just starting a new center, a needs assessment will be, well, necessary, but it is not sufficient. Classrooms, faculty, and students change, so we must be nimble in how we respond to them, which means that needs assessment is an on going process (Elliott et al., 2015). For a more detailed list of issues or questions that can be included in your process, see the multi media site associated with this book.

There is a considerable body of research that demonstrates how a needs assessment, regardless of method used, can integrate the needs of individual faculty members into the existing body of evidence-based practice (Baran, 2016; Behar-Horenstein, Garvan, Catalanotto, & Hudson-Vassell, 2014; Boman et al., 2013; Roberts, 2018). It can have other secondary benefits as well. By conducting your needs assessment, you have engaged your faculty in collaborative problem-solving, inspired the continuity of learning, and possibly started the basis of future learning communities—all tailored to your institutional context (Ng, 2015). The dissemination of the results of the needs assessment can further serve to open productive conversations with faculty groups and as a marketing and promotion tool for the work of the CTL (Hendricks, 2015).

Before you embark on your needs assessment journey, reflect for a moment on your role in the process.

> *Ask Yourself:*
> - What is your purpose or motivation for doing the needs assessment? Why do you want to (not need to) do it?
> - What is it that you'd like to find out or understand better?
> - What do you (and/or your staff) already know (or think you know) about campus needs?
> - What kinds of needs do you want to know more about? Whose needs are they?
> - What data do you have on hand, and what data do you think you might need/want to gather?

Step 1: Plan

The first step of the needs assessment planning process is determining which method(s) to use, when, and with which people or group. In this section, you will explore tools and frameworks to find out what the stakeholder groups were doing (and stopped), what stakeholders are doing, and what the stakeholders want to do.

Table 3.1 provides a brief overview of common needs assessment inputs that can be used in educational development. This list is not exhaustive, however, so you should feel free to add other sources of input as appropriate to your needs.

Based on our experience, here are a few tips and tricks to keep in mind as you plan your schedule:

- It always takes longer to collect and analyze data than we anticipate. Be mindful of the other demands on your time.
- Needs assessment data collection can be subject to ethical review, whether through an institutional review board or a related process. Be sure to check that you are following your institutional guidelines and allow time for approvals to be in place before you start.
- Be sure you give respondents or interviewees sufficient time to respond or schedule sessions. You may be under a time crunch to get this done, but you will have better responses and hear from a wider range of stakeholders with more lead time.
- Much of the subtlety in the needs assessment process comes from identifying implicit assumptions and beliefs that lurk below the surface of what is reported or said. If possible, ensure that your survey has at least one open-ended response question and that your interviews are recorded, rather than compiled by notetakers. These responses take longer to analyze (and it can be difficult to delegate that task to others), but often produce the richest insights.

TABLE 3.1

Types of Needs Assessment Input

	Description	Pros	Cons
Existing Data	Statistics and reports of community-related data	• Data already exist • Quick access • Can chart changes	• Info may be dated • Lacks people's perceptions of needs
Attitude Survey	Representative sample of population is asked to respond about issues (personal or telephone interviews, questionnaires)	• Valid data from broad range of people • Can find out behavioral info and opinions	• Can be costly • Have to build survey, which can be tricky
Key Informant	Community leaders help identify priority needs and concerns	• Quick and inexpensive • Questionnaire easy to prepare • Provides valuable contacts	• Information is likely biased by age, occupation • Few informants can represent the entire population
Group Sessions	Use group or public sessions to identify and analyze ideas, issues, and opinions	• Quick and inexpensive • Input from wide variety of people • Can aid public relations efforts • Can ask more and deeper questions to get clarity	• Attendees may not represent population • Attendees may come with negative attitude • May heighten public expectations beyond reasonable limits • Need skilled moderator

Source: Introduction to Assessing Community Needs (2013). Strengthening extension advisory leaders (SEAL). Retrieved from https://campus.extension.org/mod/page/view.php?id=26519

Step 2: Do

Now it's time to put your plan into action and collect that data. Use worksheet 3.1 to guide your needs assessment implementation.

WORKSHEET 3.1
Guide to Implementing Your Needs Assessment Process

Stakeholders [Who]	**Whose needs are being assessed?** *Individual instructors? Departments? The institution's? Faculty teaching online? Those preparing for tenure? Faculty who teach large lecture courses?*
	Who might provide insight into these needs? *Who are your stakeholders? Who can help you to understand the needs? Think about both direct stakeholders (e.g., faculty) and indirect stakeholders (e.g., students), as well as stakeholders internal and external to your unit.*
Methods [How]	**How might existing data help you?** *Do you have existing data that might shed light on these needs? How do you assess your unit's work? Might the data from program assessments be useful?*
	How might you learn more about these needs? *Surveys? Interviews? Focus groups? Strength, challenges, opportunities, threats (SCOT) analyses? Staff retreat with brainstorming? Analysis of patterns in workshop feedback?*
	How can you better understand future needs/trends? *Publications to read? Conferences to attend? Higher education trends to follow?*

Source: Chrystall & Lohe, 2015. Used with permission of the authors.

The Instrument

The most common tool for needs assessment is an electronic survey. These can get a bad rap, largely because response rates may not be as high as you want, but they can often be an efficient way to get what you need, which is input from a wide range of faculty (or other stakeholders) with relatively low investment of time and resources. Saying "a survey," however, is somewhat akin to saying "a lecture," meaning that there is no such thing as a single survey design, and survey questions afford a wide range of options and approaches. It is tempting to think you may not need to avail yourself of these options, as you can simply ask faculty what they need; however, we have found that their responses to that question are frequently less revealing or constructive that you might want (or need). The following are types of survey questions (with examples) that other educational developers have found useful in conducting their needs assessments.

Question Type 1: Baseline Satisfaction

These questions ask faculty to rate their satisfaction with the ways things currently are on campus See Figure 3.2 for an example. Among other benefits, these types of questions can help you to prioritize your programming (see chapter 5).

Question Type 2: Prioritization

Speaking of prioritization, you can simply ask your stakeholders to rate their priorities, whether by level of knowledge, desired format, interests, or other factors, as reflected in the survey questions illustrated in Figure 3.3.

Question Type 3: The Info-Question

One of the challenges in determining faculty needs is that they do not always realize what their needs are or the means that you have to meet them. You can address this problem through what we call the info-question, which serves double duty by educating your participants while simultaneously assessing their needs. For examples of info-questions, see Figure 3.4 and Table 3.2.

Figure 3.2. Survey sample.

Current College Faculty Development Activities for UFCD

Please provide your opinion of the following question about the faculty development opportunities and your participation:

✱1. Current State: Faculty Development Program

I perceive current faculty development opportunities in the UFCD program as . . .

- ○ Poor
- ○ Fair
- ○ Good
- ○ Very Good
- ○ Excellent

✱2. Participation

I perceive my current participation in faculty development activities as . . .

- ○ Never
- ○ Few (1-2/yr)
- ○ Some (3-4/yr)
- ○ Often (5-7/yr)
- ○ Frequently (8+/yr)

✱3. Mentoring

I perceive the quality of mentoring I am receiving as . . .

- ○ Poor
- ○ Fair
- ○ Good
- ○ Very Good
- ○ Excellent

4. Mentoring

If applicable, how could the mentoring you receive be improved?

Source Behar-Horenstein, L. S., Garvan, C. W., Catalanotto, F. A., & Hudson-Vassell, C. N. (2014). The role of needs assessment for faculty development initiatives. *Journal of Faculty Development, 28*(2), 75–86. Reprinted with permission.

Figure 3.3. Prioritization questions.

Teaching, Scholarship, and Leadership Skills and Priorities

Listed below are some skill and knowledge areas. First, assess your current skill/knowledge level for each area using the following scale: (1) none, (2) very little, (3) some, (4) approaching mastery, and (5) mastery/could teach others. Then, assess the corresponding level of priority you assign to each area using the following scale: (1) low, (2) medium, and (3) high.

*5. Teaching

	Please self-assess your current skill/knowledge level using the following scale:	What is the priority of this topic within your personal development?
Designing courses		
Teaching effectively		
Enhancing small group teaching		
Enhancing my classroom teaching		
Selecting appropriate teaching methods		
Using effective assessments		
Using emerging technology in the classroom		
Providing constructive feedback to learners		
Developing an educational portfolio		

Other (please specify)

*6. Scholarship

	Please self-assess your current skill/knowledge level using the following scale:	What is the priority of this topic within your personal development?
Conducting literature searches		
Documenting education outcomes		
Grantwriting in discipline research		
Developing research designs		
Writing an education manuscript		

Other (please specify)

Figure 3.4. Info-questions.

Recommendations for future programs

Please rate the following in regards to your preferred VENUES for future faculty development programming.

＊8. What are your interest levels for each of the following venues?

	Very Uninterested	Somewhat Uninterested	Neutral	Somewhat Interested	Very Interested
Faculty dialogue (informal peer-to-peer discussions about teaching over coffee)	○	○	○	○	○
Workshop (one meeting on a specific topic)	○	○	○	○	○
Institutes or retreats (full day or days)	○	○	○	○	○
Web-based resources	○	○	○	○	○
Problem-based/case-based discussions	○	○	○	○	○
Electronic networking for sharing and collaboration (discussion boards)	○	○	○	○	○
Presentations by experts outside UF	○	○	○	○	○
Seminar series (one-two hour sessions over a period of weeks)	○	○	○	○	○
Integration into department/division meetings	○	○	○	○	○

Other (please specify)

[   ]

TABLE 3.2
Info-Questions

	Very Interested	Interested	Indifferent	Not Interested	Very Disinterested
Teaching Strategies: Economizing My Effort					
Teaching Strategies: Innovative Techniques					
Diversity, Inclusion, & Accessibility in Teaching & Learning					
Student Engagement/Active Learning					
Teaching with Technology					
New Tools and Technologies for Teaching					
Support for Research, Scholarship, and Creative Work					

1. From the following list of strategic goals commonly associated with centers for teaching and learning, please rank the significance of the following goals for [insert the name of your institution] (1 is highest priority, 14 lowest):

- To support department goals, planning, and development
- To partner in the learning enterprise with libraries, technology centers, research offices, and so on
- To advance new initiative in teaching and learning
- To provide recognition and reward for excellence in teaching
- To help the institution respond to accreditation/the quality enhancement plan (QEP)
- To position the institution at the forefront of educational innovation
- To respond to critical needs as defined by the institution
- To provide support for technological tools that support teaching and learning
- To provide support for faculty members who are experiencing difficulties with their teaching
- To foster collegiality within and among faculty members and/or departments
- To act as change agents within the institution
- To respond to and support individual faculty members' goals for professional development
- To create or sustain a culture of teaching excellence
- Other (please briefly explain)

Adapted from Sorcinelli, M.D., Austin, A.E., Eddy, P.L., & Beach, A.L. (2006).

2. From the following list of emerging ideas or tools in teaching and learning, please *rank* your current *knowledge of* and *interest in learning more* about each item (10 is the highest interest, 1 the least):

- Problem-based learning—a student-centered model in which students learn about a subject through the experience of solving an open-ended problem
- Universal design for learning—a learning science framework that seeks to optimize teaching and learning for all learners in all settings
- High-impact practices—a collection of practices (e.g., undergraduate research) with proven track records for increasing student engagement
- Contemplative pedagogy—a cross-disciplinary model that uses a number of techniques to create deeper levels of awareness, concentration, or insight in your students

- Threshold pedagogy—a learning science model in which students learn to overcome cognitive bottlenecks to greater depth of disciplinary understanding
- Competency-based pedagogy—usually self-paced, online, or hybrid modules in which students receive multiple chances to demonstrate that they have mastered core competencies
- Flipped pedagogy—hybrid model in which students master content knowledge outside of class (usually on-line) and focus on higher-order problem solving in the classroom
- Virtual worlds—in this digital model, the next generation of 3D technology allows students to become immersed and to interact within 3D virtual worlds (e.g., Google Cardboard, Microsoft Hololens)
- Gamification—in this interactive digital model, students are motivated to learn using competitive, cumulative, quest-based, or other strategies that include reward systems

Question Type 4: Thick Description

Qualitative researchers will tell you that one of the best ways to elicit more meaningful responses is not to ask a direct question, but rather to ask the respondents to please describe something about their lives or their work. An added bonus would be including statements that start with "I." Most of us like to tell stories about ourselves, and you can harness that tendency toward deeper insight.

If you could add just ONE program, initiative, approach, project, or similar professional development opportunity, and you wanted that program to make the biggest impact on the culture of faculty development and teaching and learning here at [insert name of institution], what program would you want to see added? Please briefly describe and explain your choice.

As a teacher, I would benefit from:

As a scholar, I would benefit from:

As a member of the [insert name of institution] campus community, I would benefit from:

Please (briefly) describe a recent class session in which you believed that the students learned a great deal. What were the secrets of your success?

Please (briefly) describe a recent class session that you believed did not lead to effective student learning. What do you think were the challenges or obstacles?

Question Type 5: Overcoming Obstacles

You can also use your needs assessment process to identify, and potentially address or overcome, potential obstacles (e.g., availability, interest, recognition, or communication) to participation.

Availability: Select the days and times you are most available to attend faculty development events

	Monday	Tuesday	Wednesday	Thursday	Friday	Saturday	Sunday
Morning							
Noon							
Afternoon							
Evening							

How often have you attended a faculty development event?

- Often
- Sometimes
- Rarely
- Never

What are your reasons for not attending? (Select *all* that apply)

- Scheduled time of event was inconvenient
- Topics did not match my learning needs
- No monetary compensation for attending

- Attendance is not required
- Lack of notification of the event/s
- Notified too late
- Other:_____

How are you notified of faculty development events? (Select *all* that apply)

- Email notifications
- Faculty development website
- Program director communications
- Flyers mailed to my home
- Flyers provided in my mailbox
- Word-of-mouth from fellow adjunct faculty

What is your preferred way to be notified of faculty development events? (Select *all* that apply)

- Email notifications
- Faculty development website
- Program director communications
- Flyers mailed to my home
- Flyers provided in my mailbox
- Word-of-mouth from fellow adjunct faculty

Questions used with permissions of the authors.

Step 3: Analyze

You've planned your process, collected your data, and now you have a great big steaming pile of it right there on your desktop. Yup. You sure do. Right there. A lot of it. Uh, huh. It's time to take it to the next step, which is to analyze and make sense of what you've got. It's very possible that not all of it is useful. It is simultaneously just as possible that all of it is equally useful. Here are some strategies to turn that pile into something productive.

- *Prioritize.* From what you've seen so far, what sources of data are most likely to bear fruit? Which are your low-hanging fruit (i.e., easy and quick to get results) and which will require the most effort (pages of open-ended, uncoded text or even worse [shudder] audio files that need to be transcribed in order to become pages of open-ended, uncoded text)? Which sources do you really need in order to move forward, and which do you simply want to showcase your work effectively?

- *Look for gaps.* We're sure that you were thorough when you made your plan and collected your data, but it is likely that either you couldn't realize every part of your plan or you learned something along the way that evoked new questions. Look over what you have and ask yourself, What's missing? What else do I need to ensure that I am as responsive as possible?

- *Analyze.* A discussion of effective social science research methods is beyond the scope of this book, but be sure that you follow appropriate standards, as this adds to your credibility.

- *Present.* Your needs assessment, when distributed, serves partly as a teaching tool for you and your CTL colleagues as well for your stakeholders. Think about how you present the information in a way that will get the results you want and for a wide audience. For your readers who are not social scientists, for example, it can be helpful to provide visualizations (e.g., graphs) or "nuggets" (i.e., short summaries) of the most salient results in addition to detailed statistical presentations. If you want to add a little literary flair, it is becoming increasingly common to include narratives, or evocative stories and pictures, to help paint the picture of what your faculty want, and how you can give them what they need.

Step 4: Act

Congratulations, you've done it. Take a moment and pat yourself on the back Your needs assessment is complete, and that's not an easy feat. You can take only a moment, however, because needs assessment is only one step in the larger strategic planning process.

In the next chapter, we will talk about how to use the results of your needs assessment to shape your long-term goals; in other words, to use what they need to get where you want to be.

And you really can't rest on your laurels even after you've completed the process, as faculty needs are always changing (Elliott et al., 2015). At the same time, our assessment tools and methods are growing more sophisticated, allowing us to go further in addressing the gap between implicit and explicit expectations, between necessary and sufficient conditions for change, and between what your campus has and what it needs to reach its aspirations. And those aspirations are distinctive. Your needs assessment may suggest common solutions that are supported in the educational development literature: workshops, learning communities, course (re)designs, consultations, and more.

That being said, our shift to organizational development means that we are adapting what we do to suit the needs of our distinctive institutions. Research has shown that community college instructors need ways to connect programs to those who need them the most (Maxwell & Kazlauskas, 1992); faculty at small colleges seek to teach in ways that closely align with their institutional ethos (Mooney & Reder, 2008; Reder, 2007); researchers at doctoral-granting institutions yearn to discover the next big breakthrough in learning science; and professors at regional comprehensive institutions crave integration among teaching, research, and service (Crow et al., 2018). And there are differences by discipline, rank, setting, size—the level of granularity may even come down to individual character traits. Your needs assessment will not look like anyone else's, and although you may never be able to capture all of the nuances and variances of your campus perfectly, if you try and you try (and you keep trying), you can find personal and professional satisfaction.

4

THE BIG ASK

What Will You Ask For?

"Will you create my center?" If you have been tasked with starting a new center, or resurrecting a defunct one, then you will have to face the challenge we call "the big ask." Not unlike getting down on one knee with a ring in hand, this is where you make your strongest case for the people, space, resources, and other items you will need in order to be able to successfully start your new life as a center. The big ask may take the form of a formal document or grand gesture, but, unlike a marriage proposal, it can also take the form of a series of artifacts or pitches to a number of different audiences or offices. You can think of the big ask not so much as a moment in time, but rather a process of marshaling your evidence, crafting your strategy, and putting your best foot forward.

The big ask can be a very daunting task. If you are starting a new center, then you will not have precedent to go by, and if you are revitalizing a center you may want to be careful not to directly emulate the defunct model. This is why establishing your baseline and conducting your needs assessment (covered in chapters 2 and 3) can be critical to your success. There are aspects of the big ask, such as finances and staffing, that many faculty moving into educational development positions lack experience with, and the ability to effectively apply strategies in negotiating for space, money, and positions is a skill that takes time (and wisdom) to hone. If it helps, you will get better at these over time and you will likely find yourself at one of your strongest negotiating points when you first start (or restart) your center and have momentum on your side.

It can also be daunting for us to provide you with models and advice, as the big ask is often very context specific, in not only its content (what you ask for) but also the process(es) by which you will ask for it (Kezar & Eckel, 2002). A common strategy for those looking to establish a new center is to ask directors of established (and admired) centers for examples. Although a sound approach in many respects, this strategy can also be discouraging, as established centers have had longer than you to build up staff and resources, and it is not uncommon for long-established centers to have lost their big ask documents (and institutional memories) to the mists of time, or to have documents that are less relevant to the current conditions within higher education. As much as possible, you may wish to reach out to CTLs that have the most in common with the roles and responsibilities you envision for your own, which may or may not be the same as those of your identified peer institutions.

In the following sections, we will do our best to prepare you for your own version of the big ask, largely by giving you a better sense of the kinds of things you should be asking for. Big ask topics are among the most requested by those who are starting or revitalizing new CTLs, and so we have compiled the most common issues and organized them into the following categories: people, space, resources, infrastructure (e.g, furniture, carpet, copiers), and other affordances.

Your People

How many people do you need to staff your CTL effectively? There's not an easy answer to that question, as staffing levels are often a function of local institutional and budgetary conditions and the solution is sensitive to what responsibilities you are being asked to, or are choosing to, undertake. Several of us on the Taking Flight team have heard the informal rule of thumb that a CTL should have full-time support person roughly 1 per 5,000 full-time equivalents (FTEs; student enrollment), but we were unable to locate a source or corroborating evidence for this ratio. Anecdotally, the ratio seems to have some validity, if you count only those staff members who work on traditional teaching and learning support. The number increases with additional responsibilities, especially in the areas of educational technology and distance education.

What kinds of staff members should you ask for? Although a systematic study of staffing for CTLs has not been conducted in recent years, previous studies indicate that there are some conventional roles and relationships that have emerged from the history of CTLs (Sorcinelli et al., 2006). Most established centers are led by a *director* (or equivalent title), who may also hold additional titles, such as assistant dean or associate provost. The POD Network membership survey data strongly suggest that most directors serve in full-time positions, but part-time directors remain a significant presence in the field, especially in smaller schools (Collins-Brown, Cruz, & Torosyan, 2016).

The director may be supported by one or more *associate* or *assistant directors*, positions that reflect our historical emphasis on creating pathways for career development, such as a line of succession from assistant to associate to director. There are some indications that these hierarchical structures may be giving way to more flexible and open organizational structures as CTLs move away from a primary emphasis on the provision of services, but a clear alternative model has yet to emerge in practice (Gravett & Bernhagen, 2015). Center staff may also include full-time *consultants*, a title that reflects their role in working directly with faculty, as well as titles like *subdirector* or *project manager*. If the center is integrated with other areas of academic life, such as educational technology or a writing center, there will also be staff associated with these, and the roles for these positions tend to follow their own naming conventions, for example, instructional designer. In their Faculty Development Center Matrix, the American Council on Education does not specify positions by number or name but rather suggests that high performing centers have a "generous" ratio of staff to FTEs, and that "staffing is adequate to meet and *create* demand for services" (emphasis added) (Haras, Ginsberg, Magruder, & Zakrajsek, 2019).

We also recommend that you consider the level of administrative support you may need and include a person (or people) who receive visitors, perform clerical tasks, and oversee budgetary transactions. CTLs with heavy event schedules may also be fortunate to include an event planner, or other support person with significant responsibilities in this area. Other less common, but often desirable, positions may include a data analyst, researcher/research support, assessment coordinator, technical support, lab/studio manager, and subject matter or disciplinary specialists (e.g., STEM education; diversity and inclusion). If you find yourself taking on all these roles yourself, take some solace in knowing that you are not alone in that position. Some of the most successful CTLs in the United States started out, and some have even remained, centers of one.

Keep in mind, too, that your staff may include more than just the people on your permanent payroll. With a growing emphasis on students as cocreators and coresearchers in teaching and learning, it can be invaluable to include students in your staff, whether through work-study, internships, or paid positions. The hiring of *graduate student assistants* can extend your staffing, and they can be highly effective at designing and implementing programming aimed toward their peers. A number of CTLs also maintain *faculty fellows* programs, in which selected faculty are hired and/or selected, usually on a fixed-term basis, to provide service to the CTL. Although the intent of a fellows program is primarily to develop the abilities of the fellow (rather than extend your staff per se), these positions can often serve to extend your outreach and advocacy capabilities (Shinnar & Williams, 2008; D. L. Wright, 2002).

Figure 4.1. Organizational chart, Center for Excellence in Learning and Teaching, Iowa State University.

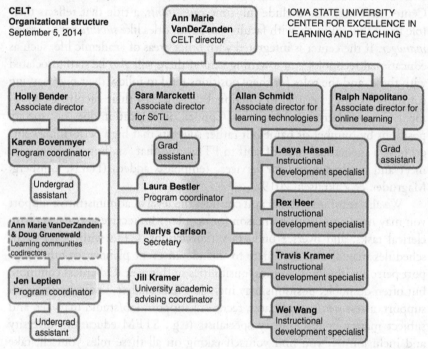

The organizational charts in Figures 4.1 to 4.4 provide some examples of distinctive models for CTL staffing. Please note that these examples are drawn from larger CTLs. This is not intended to diminish the value of smaller CTLs. Rather, it is reflective of the fact that smaller CTLs do not often provide separate organizational charts on their public websites.

Figure 4.2. Organizational chart, The Teaching Center at Washington University, St. Louis, 2018.

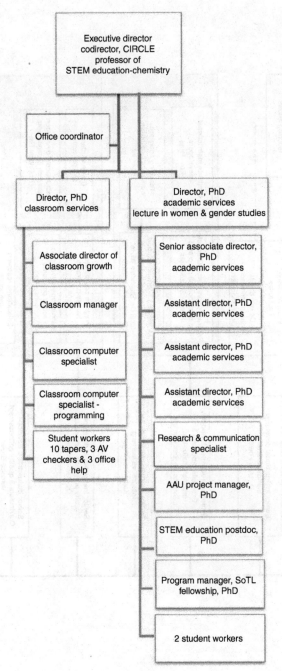

Figure 4.3. Organizational chart, Center for Teaching Excellence, University of Ottawa.

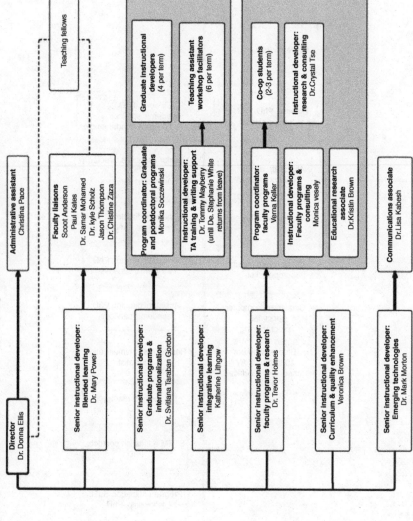

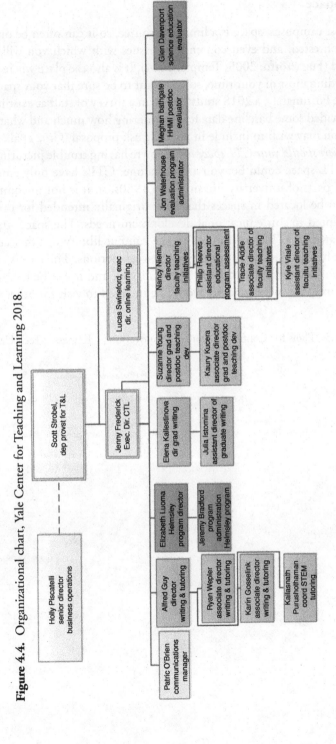

Figure 4.4. Organizational chart, Yale Center for Teaching and Learning 2018.

Your Space

On most campuses, space is a limited resource, so it can often be one of the most contested, and even contentious, issues with which you will have to contend (Fugazzotto, 2009; Temple, 2014). It is also the place where you will be spending most of your time, so you want to be sure that your space works for you. Fortunately, a 2018 study based on a survey of staff at existing CTLs has provided some baseline data for considering how much and what kind of space you may wish to include in your big ask proposal (Cruz et al., 2019).

Where should your CTL space be? If you're having trouble picturing where your CTL space could be, you are not alone. CTLs have only emerged as integral parts of university life since the 1980s, so it is not uncommon for CTLs to be located in spaces that were originally intended for other uses and adapted to suit educational development needs. The space study suggests that most CTLs are located in the campus library or other academic support buildings. This location serves two functions. The first is convenience—you want faculty to be able to find you, and it can be helpful to be located in spaces where faculty would be inclined to visit for other reasons.

Figure 4.5. Plans for Center for Teaching Innovation at Tennessee Tech University (2015).

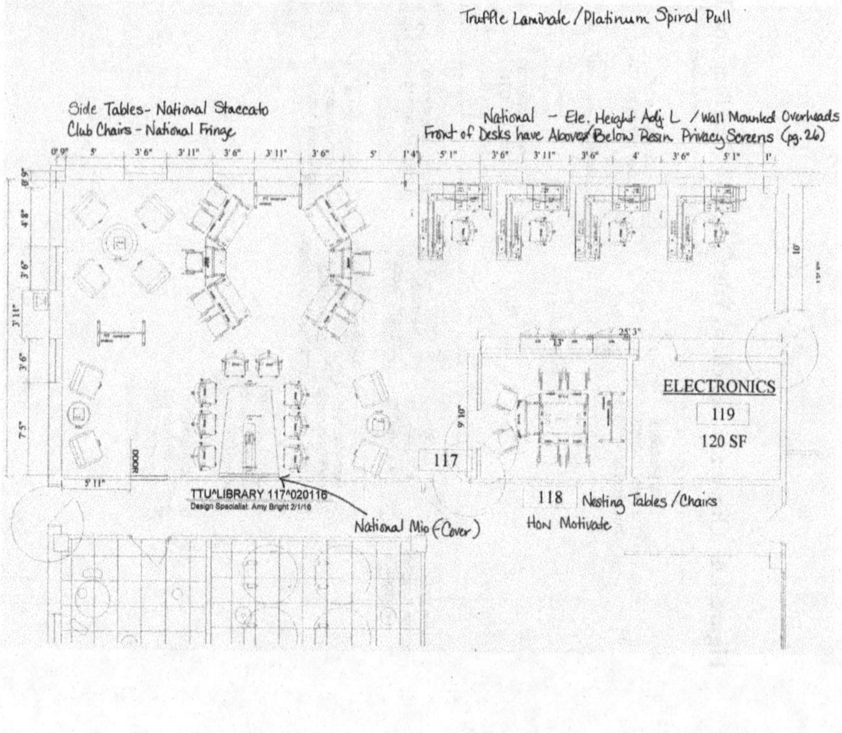

Figure 4.6. Center map, Center for Teaching and Learning, Paradise Valley Community College.

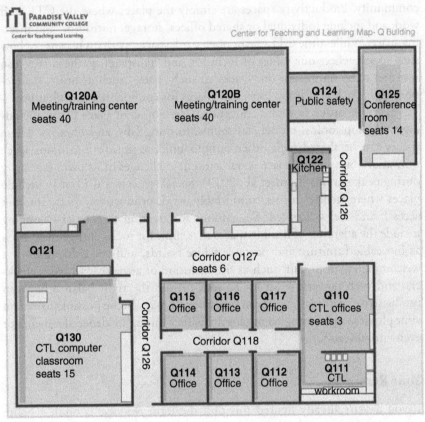

The second is symbolic—the more central your location, the more you signal to your campus stakeholders that faculty development is a priority of the institution. At the University of Virginia, for example, the Center for Teaching Excellence is located right on the institution's fabled lawn, and at South Seattle Community College, the Teaching and Learning Center is adjacent to the campus's highest point, the clock tower. The relative size of the CTL can also be symbolic, but the study revealed considerable variation in square footage across institutions, with a very ballpark average around 1,500-3,000 square feet (Cruz et al., 2019). It is interesting to note that as faculty themselves become less tethered to the physical campus, whether because of campus expansions or technology-mediated instruction, we may be asked to revisit how we see our own spaces in the near future (Donnelli-Sallee, Dailey-Hebert, & Mandernach, 2012).

What kinds of space should you have in your CTL? The CTL space study identified three primary purposes for CTL space: productivity, learning, and community. Productivity spaces are simply the places where the CTL staff work and include individual or shared offices, storage, restrooms, and meeting space. While some CTLs favor open work spaces, perhaps because of how such spaces reflect our values of inclusion and transparency, the survey also revealed some significant drawbacks to such spaces, such as noise, distraction, and a lack of privacy, especially places for confidential consultations.

Learning space is where educational development takes place, including workshop rooms, model classrooms, learning labs, and libraries. These spaces can be shared with other campus units to ensure maximum space utilization, but sharing space is not without challenges of its own, especially during peak periods (Cruz et al., 2019). Social space in a CTL may include places where faculty can sit comfortably, work productively (e.g., Internet access), and feel welcomed. Suggestions for creating a sense of belonging include the adaption of flexible spaces that allow for social engagement, such as moveable furniture and portable white boards, and the cultivation of a welcoming environment, such as the inclusion of attractive art, coffeemakers, and even flowers. Most CTLs seek to find the right balance between productivity, learning, and social functions. It may also be possible to extend your physical space using technology, whether through videoconferencing or even virtual reality.

Your Resources

If you haven't already figured this out, the term *resources* is often a polite way to imply financial support—money—though it can include in-kind or other forms of support as well. As part of your big ask, you will most likely be asked to propose a budget for your CTL. New CTL directors frequently want to know how much they should ask for, and they tend to be disappointed with our responses. It is nearly impossible for us to provide a dollar figure that takes into account the myriad of contingencies that apply to institutional budgets. You may want to ask existing units on your campus of similar size and scope if they might share their budget information with you, as this may be a stronger indicator of what is possible given the situational factors you face.

What we can do, though, is give you some sense of what is being asked for, assuming you are being given the opportunity to manage your own budget (which you should definitely ask for). Most independent academic units, such as CTLs, have something akin to an *operating budget*, for example, recurring funds that are used to keep you in operation. This budget may include items such as office supplies, copies and copier fees, phone charges, postage, equipment maintenance, licensing fees, subscriptions, memberships, and sometimes even utility bills. These expenses can accumulate fast and do not always follow the same fiscal cycle as the university, so they require careful management.

You may also wish to ask for an additional budget line, or extension of your operating budget, to cover common categories of expenses for CTLs. This may include fees for conference *travel* and professional development for you and your staff, if such expenses are not already covered by other university funds outside of the CTL. Most CTLs also maintain a linked or separate budget that covers expenses related to their programming and events, especially for those events that are fee generating or sponsor supported. The good news is that many staples of educational development, such as workshops or faculty learning communities, can be implemented with little to no budget, while others, such as conferences or visiting scholars, may require a more substantial financial outlay. The Taking Flight team recommends that you pay attention to the fiscal calendar; as many educational developments occur over the summer, we often find ourselves awkwardly straddling two annual cycles.

Your event and programming budget may include funds that go directly to faculty. The use of stipends and grants to incentivize faculty to engage in transforming their teaching and learning practice has met with mixed reviews in practice. While recent research has shown that course redesign grants can be very effective motivators (M. C. Wright, Cook, & Brady, 2000), the practice of paying faculty to, say, attend a summer institute is a precedent you may wish to consider carefully before you set it. On one hand, research on faculty motivation suggests that most are not primarily motivated by money (or similar extrinsic rewards) (Wergin, 2001), but on the other hand, the availability of funding can often signal the university's investment, or commitment, to teaching transformation. You should be sure (or as sure as you can be), however, that if you set the expectation, you will be able to continue to provide such funding in the future. Some special circumstances may apply. Many faculty at four-year schools operate under nine-month contracts, so they may see time spent in the summer as outside of that contract and, therefore, appropriate for additional payment. Some institutions also subsidize adjunct faculty (usually on an hourly basis) to participate in faculty development, as their regular salaries may be insufficient to cover time spent.

Fixed assets, such as computers and office furniture, often follow different budgetary processes than operating budgets. Most often, these funds are granted as single, nonrecurring requests, although you may wish to consider adding recurring funds for updating or maintenance if this option is available. If you are looking to make a proposal to cover the costs of furniture, your university likely has identified a preferred vendor or vendors, and your sales representative will be eager to provide you with a quote. Most office furniture companies have interior designers on staff, too, who can help you with layouts, colors, and materials if desired. Technology requests, such as computers, tablets, monitors/screens, telecomm devices, webcams, and more, will also likely come from preferred vendors through established request processes. Even if you are not required to do so, the Taking Flight team recommends reaching out to your information technology (IT) office, as they may be asked to install, support, and maintain your technology pieces in the future.

An increasing number of CTLs are looking at sources of financial support to supplement those provided directly by the institution; and these separate funding streams often require that you maintain separate budget lines. Such forms of support may include external grants, whether from government sources, such as National Science Foundation (NSF) programs; major educational foundations, such as Lumina, Gates, or Spencer; or state and regional foundations. Other CTLs are fortunate to have received endowment funds, which may be attached to naming opportunities (e.g., the Schreyer Institute for Teaching Excellence at Penn State). Some directors have experimented with other forms of donations and directed funds (Shaker & Palmer, 2012), and you are encouraged to engage your office of development to investigate options that may be available to you.

Other Affordances

When you are first starting out, it can be tempting to focus on what is immediately in front of you, such as an empty room with no furniture or staff, rather than other perhaps less tangible goals. Sometimes referred to as "putting out fires" mode, this can lead to a focus on the short term over the long term, including an emphasis on limited programming over broader transformation. You certainly can't function without, say, a desk or electricity, but you may not be able to function as effectively if you don't negotiate for certain affordances, or essential aspects of your operating environment, as part of your big ask.

For example, you may be thinking about your own organizational chart, as mentioned previously, but you should also consider your own reporting line. If your reporting line has not already been established for you, consider asking for where you would like it to be. Support from senior administration is an essential part of the success of a new CTL, and you will want to have as strong a support as you possibly can, from the highest office possible. It can be tempting to suggest a reporting line based on the interests and qualities of individual leaders, but you are building a CTL that you intend to last for decades, well beyond the tenure of a single senior administrator. CTLs commonly report to an academic leader, such as a provost or an associate provost, but there is considerable variation in practice; the right fit will depend on how closely aligned your CTL's goals are with those of the office to which you report. Integrated CTLs, such as those that include educational technology or distance education, may find themselves faced with the possibility of multiple reporting lines (e.g., direct or dotted line report to a CIO or dean for distance education), a situation that can bring you double the advocacy, but also twice the headaches.

Related to your reporting line, you may also choose to ask for access to key people or committees that will enable you to serve as an effective agent of change or faculty advocate. Later in this volume, we will present you with strategies for getting "a seat at the table" once your center has been established (Siering et al., 2015), but you can include representation as part of your big ask as well. If you need to have regular communication with your chief academic officer so that they can support your efforts effectively, then include regular meeting sessions in your proposal. Numerous CTL directors have spoken about the importance of engaging with faculty governance bodies, such as senates or unions, and how even limited access to their proceedings can inform what you do. Ask to be included. If you believe you would have reason to want to access the deans of the academic colleges, ask for a dedicated place on the docket of the council of deans, or representation on the general education advisory board, or regular updates to the IT council, or dedicated space on the university's main website. If you establish your presence at the onset, you can save yourself the trouble of having to elbow your way onto the table later.

Just as you may wish to ask to be represented, you may also ask to have others represented. You are likely to have a faculty advisory board for your CTL, for example, and if you want to ensure that that board is as representative of campus feedback as possible, then you will want to see all constituencies represented—even those that may not be as enthusiastic or as interested in faculty development as the others. This is a somewhat roundabout way of saying that if you have a college or department that may be reluctant to support your services, then you can ask for formal support in bringing them to your table.

In addition to asking for reporting and representation, you may want to consider articulating foundational policies. You may also consider adding a diversity and inclusion statement to your big ask proposal. These statements may lay out clearly for whom your CTL provides services. For example, adjunct faculty, graduate students, geographically dispersed faculty, and other underrepresented constituents may not realize that you would be happy to work with them unless you say so. Also, these statements reflect your commitment to the principles and values of diversity and inclusion. The following are a few examples of such statements:

The Sheridan Center supports an inclusive learning environment where diverse perspectives are recognized, respected, and seen as a source of strength.
—Sheridan Center for Teaching and Learning [cocurricular statement], Brown University

Recognize the integral value of diverse perspectives and inclusive teaching approaches; strive to ensure that all faculty, teaching assistants, and students, regardless of their identity, can excel.
—Center for Teaching Excellence, Texas A&M University

Sustain inclusive learning environments where students feel a sense of belongingness and can thrive.
Diversity is one of five key synergistic and often interdependent domains—along with innovation, evidence-based teaching, technology, and assessment & evaluation—that guide the resources, services, and mission of the CTI.
Our classrooms reflect our increasingly diverse society. As Cornell promotes teaching and learning environments with verve, we benefit from an intentional process of exploration and application of strategies drawn from social and educational research, neuroscience, and our collective experiences. Our programs, through a process of interdisciplinary collegial reflection and discernment, serve to share diverse perspectives, knowledge, and teaching practices.
—Center for Teaching Innovation, Cornell University

As we advance in rank and administrative responsibility we often think our shoulders are broader than they really are. Educational developers are notoriously devoted to individual and institutional success and have a hard time saying "no." But it is important to know our strengths and weaknesses and to realize that it's simply not possible—or wise—to "fake it til you make it," especially with regard to diversity, equity, and inclusion. Although it is our collective responsibility to constantly learn and grow in this regard, it is also wise to consider ways to fold expertise into your CTL. This may come in the form of partnerships with existing units with whom we can sponsor joint programs or in the form of faculty associates or fellows with expertise in diversity and inclusion.

Another affordance that can be included in your big ask is support for your confidentiality policy or statement. Confidentiality has emerged as a best practice for CTLs, and a confidentiality policy can demonstrate to faculty that you are creating a safe space for them to discuss sensitive issues, that they can confidently take risks in their teaching practice, and that you respect their right to privacy (Huston & Weaver, 2008; Meyer & Evans, 2005; Taylor, Colet, Saroyan, Frenay, 2012). The extent to which confidentiality can be extended to your clients in the CTL is often dependent on your local context, and in extreme situations, you may need to rely upon the confidentiality statement to support your actions. To be proactive in these situations means clarifying the limitations and exceptions to that policy/statement from the beginning so that you can communicate this to your faculty and to those who may request information about your faculty that violates that confidentiality. The Taking Flight team recommends that you share drafts of your confidentiality policy with your university's legal counsel to ensure that it is in keeping

Figure 4.7. Confidentiality policy, Coulter Faculty Commons, Western Carolina University.

Records that are created, received, or maintained by the Coulter Faculty Commons are confidential personnel records. Such records pertain to professional development and teaching effectiveness and are for internal Commons purposes. The records are confidential and will not be disclosed to third parties unless disclosure is required by law or the faculty member consents to the disclosure of records by signing a written authorization. Such records will not be used for tenure, reappointment, promotion, or disciplinary purposes without the faculty member's consent. However, the department head and dean together can authorize administrative review in certain limited circumstances where the disclosure of records is essential to maintain the integrity of the department or university (for example, investigations involving fraud or misrepresentation)

Figure 4.8. Confidentiality policy, Center for Teaching, Vanderbilt University

The Center for Teaching is a university-wide resource for the Vanderbilt teaching community. Its goals are to promote excellence in teaching through dialogue, inquiry and research, and to offer teachers feedback and an opportunity for reflection on their teaching. To fulfill these goals, the Center must offer a trustworthy environment to those it serves, and thus has established the following policies. These policies were created by the Center's faculty advisory board with representation from all of Vanderbilt's schools, and are also supported by the Ethical Guidelines for Educational Developers developed by the national POD Network in Higher Education. Please address any questions or concerns to the Center's director.

Teachers can receive feedback on their teaching through the Center for Teaching in a variety of ways: small group analyses (SGAs), videotaping, class observations, microteaching, conversations about particular teaching challenges, or other consultation sessions.

The Center is dedicated to providing teachers with these opportunities to observe themselves and their students in a confidential manner, for formative purposes, without risk of evaluation or censure. Therefore:

- The Center will gather feedback (videotape, SGA, etc.) about a course only upon the request of the teacher.
- The Center does not make feedback information available to anyone except the teacher.
- The Center expects that consultation on a videotape will occur first between a Center consultant and the teacher. The Center recognizes that teachers may benefit further by subsequently sharing the videotape with their colleagues, and they may do so at their own discretion.
- Feedback gathered and/or given by the Center is meant to be formative, and thus is not intended to be used in promotion, tenure, or reappointment processes.
- The Center will release the name of a participant only upon his or her request. At the request of a participant, the Center will provide written verification of participation listing the type(s) of activity, date(s) and Center consultant(s). Such "certificates of participation" may be included in tenure and promotion files, or used for other evaluative processes.
- Occasionally, the Center may ask for a teacher's written permission to show another individual or group an excerpt of a videotape or other material to illustrate a particular teaching issue.
- The Center periodically consults with schools and departments on ways of improving the teaching done by, and the mentoring of, graduate student teaching assistants. In this capacity, the Center shares models and ideas, raises questions, and otherwise advises—but is not or enforcing TA teaching requirements.

—Confidentiality policy, Center for Teaching, Vanderbilt University with university standards, and then post the policy/statement publicly, preferably in multiple places. See Figure 4.7 and Figure 4.8 for sample CTL confidentiality statements.

Once you have developed your big ask, it's now time to take it out to your stakeholders, even those who are not in a position, at least not directly, to grant your requests, so that the proposal comes not just from one suitor, but from many. It can be helpful to set expectations early (including yours) because it is unlikely that you will get everything you ask for; but it is even more unlikely that you will get what you want if you do not ask. You can think of this process as an opportunity for you to practice your skills as an agent of change. Even the most seasoned administrators can benefit from developing the often subtle and distinctive processes, practices, and relationships that support effective leadership in educational development.

5

STRATEGIC PLANNING

How Will You Define Your Path?

Are you a hedgehog or a fox? According to philosopher Isaiah Berlin, the world can be divided into two kinds of people, those who pursue many activities at the same time, like a fox who tries many different tricks to capture an elusive prey, or those who focus on doing one thing well, like the hedgehog whose prickly spine thwarts the fox every time. The lesson of the so-called hedgehog principle, according to management consultant Jim Collins (2001), is to focus on what you do best; this can, in turn, allow you to do more than just survive, but to have lasting impact. It is how, in his words, you can go from being good to great (Collins, 2001). The primary tool for implementing the hedgehog principle is strategic planning, a multifaceted process that results in the creation of a long-term strategic plan that includes the articulation of the mission, vision, and strategic goals for your CTL.

As we make our shift to organizational development, CTLs are expected to be more than service providers; they should contribute to the cultivation of a campus culture that promotes excellence in teaching and learning. We do this in myriad ways, often assuming different identities: We are administrators, staff, and/or faculty; we are instructional designers and course (re) designers; we are "the people who run all those workshops," learning communities, and SoTL initiatives; and we are faculty developers. Sometimes we are all of these things and switch hats depending on the issue before us, and other times we are part of a team that covers all of the bases. The fact of the matter is that CTLs come in all shapes and sizes: Some have dialed-in divisions of labor and sometimes you *are* the CTL. Regardless, in order to build a successful CTL, it is essential to develop, in sequence, an authentic identity, an institutionally aligned vision and mission, and a plan for how you intend to get there. In short, it is necessary to become a mighty fine hedgehog.

Step 1: Finding Your Hedgehog

Finding your hedgehog, or primary focus, is the cornerstone of your strategic planning process. Jim Collins (2005) suggests four leading questions to help (nonprofit) organizations find their hedgehog, and Bruce Kelley has posed these in the context of educational development:

> 1. What are the brutal facts?

> This is an honest appraisal of who we are and the situation we find ourselves in. . . . Few educational developers have a permanent seat on their institution's executive committee, few of our centers have an overabundance of personnel and money, and few of us have the institutional authority to mandate major policy changes. Beyond that, however, we all have our individual brutal facts to face. (Kelley, 2018)

> 2. What drives our resource engine?

> We operate under a "resource engine" rather than an economic one. Our resources include our budget, facilities, time, and personnel. What drives our resource engine is typically a combination of reputation, perceived need, and documented impact. A CTL that has established a reputation for excellence, fulfills a perceived need, and is able to document impact is less likely to have its resources assigned to another campus entity. (Kelley, 2018)

> 3. What are we/can we be the best at?

> A Hedgehog Concept is not a goal to be the best, a strategy to be the best, an intention to be the best, a plan to be the best. It is an *understanding* of what you *can* be the best at . . . In the end, therefore, this idea is not about competition but of understanding the unique nature of each of our centers. (Kelley, 2018)

> 4. What are we passionate about?

> If our passion is aligned with what we believe we can be best in the world at, and if it helps drive our resource engine, then it can produce powerful results. If our passion is not aligned within the hedgehog concept, however, we are unlikely to move from good to great. (Kelley, 2018)

Your hedgehogs can be very straightforward. At Penn State, for example, the CTL chose three simple, but powerful, words to capture the foundations of their strategic plan: visibility, interaction, and quality. In the context of educational development, your hedgehogs could be compared to the concept of enduring understanding that underlie Wiggins, Wiggins, and McTighes's understanding by design process (2005). In other words, your hedgehogs are not just things that are nice for you to do, or even important that you do (and know how to do), but rather they are those components that are central to your sustained existence (Wiggins et al., 2005).

Step 2: Mission Control

This second connection carries with it the temptation to equate course design and strategic planning, a temptation that you should probably try to resist, as the two have different purposes, processes, and outcomes (Hines, 2009; Weinstein, Linse, & Brua, 2011). Strategic planning consists of three primary components: developing a vision of who you are and wish to be; a mission that identifies and guides your efforts; and strategies you will deploy to accomplish them, including goals and processes (Rubin, 2007). If you are starting a new center or revitalizing an existing one, creating your strategic plan will likely be one of your first responsibilities.

The following exercises are designed to guide you and your team through the process of developing a consensual, compelling, and authentic strategic plan. Although each component is addressed discretely in an effort to generate mutually exclusive categories, the relationships between and among topics should be regarded as the glue that unites your efforts. As is evidenced in Figure 5.1, these topics are interrelated.

Figure 5.1. Components of a CTL strategic plan.

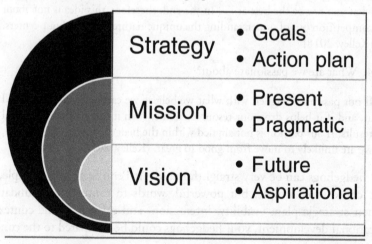

Your Vision Statement

A vision statement is a short statement, usually only a sentence or two, that defines the aspirations you have for the CTL. The most important feature of a vision statement is that it inspires; it needs to motivate you, the other members of your CTL, and your allies and stakeholders, to want to achieve what it promises. Inadequate vision statements are too broad or ambiguous to be meaningful, too ambitious to seem doable, or too narrowly focused to seem relevant to everyone.

Ask Yourself:

To contemplate your vision statement, you may want to ask questions such as the following:

- What would your institution be like if your center was no longer needed?
- How would you describe your institution if your center achieved its mission?
- What would faculty and students be doing if your success rate was 100%?

Source: Linse, 2018; Weinstein et al., 2011

Your Mission Statement

Your mission statement is the anchor of your strategic plan and the standard to which you will be held accountable. It should describe what you do all day, every day, as simply part of doing what you do. A good mission statement is ambitious yet reasonable, effectively balancing internal and external expectations in an authentic voice that resonates on your campus.

Ask Yourself:

To develop your mission statement, you may want to ask questions such as the following:

- Why do you exist?
- What work do you do?
- How do you spend your time?

Source: Weinstein et al., 2011

From there, mission statements often contain stock components: who you are, what you do, for whom you do it, and how you do it (or will do it), which results in a certain formulaic quality in how they are presented. You can look at the following template as a potential guideline, but do not feel constrained by the structure. Your mission statement is for and about you, so you should use whatever format works.

Mission Statement Template:

As [who you are], our mission is to [what you do] for [whom you do it] by [how you do it] so that [why].

For examples of mission statements from other CTLs, see the multimedia site associated with *Taking Flight*.

As you and your team work through these exercises, bear in mind that the vision is typically aspirational and future focused while the mission asserts what you will do in the here and now. Your vision represents who you are as a center as well what you wish—realistically and in the context of your duties and institutional setting—to become. You may not, yet, be an internationally recognized center, but you may realistically have the credibility to strive for that. You may presently be more aligned with the university than an agent of change within it, but you can (and should) strive for that. And you should think about your mission in the context of that vision but be mindful of the instrumental rationality of establishing and accomplishing tangible goals (Drake et al., 2012).

Step 3: Mission Accomplished?

The third part of your strategic plan is the strategies you will use to get you to where you want to go; these include identifying your short-term and long-term goals, and then establishing the people, resources, and benchmarks associated with each of those goals.

Ask Yourself:
To develop your strategic goals, you may want to ask questions such as the following:

- How will you know that you have achieved your mission?
- How will you know you are being effective or successful?
- What about your unit's work could be improved? How? By how much?

Source: Weinstein et al., 2011

Once you have your mission statement goals clearly articulated, you can then start to think about how you will accomplish them. Using the following fields, identify what your CTL will do, how it will do it, and how success will be measured.

Using Worksheet 5.1, clearly identify your strategies, including time tables, people, and milestones for each goal. If you want to say "mission accomplished!" you need to know what completion looks like, and if it is an iterative process of working toward enduring goals—and much of educational development is enduring—you should specify how you will mark your progress and use data to inform your next steps. In strategic planning, waypoints are commonly used like mile markers to indicate our progress toward defined end points. Map them out. Be ambitious but realistic—set yourself up for success, not failure.

Ask Yourself:

- Do you have a vision statement for your CTL?   Y / N
- Do you have a mission statement for your CTL?   Y / N
- Do you have a set of strategic goals for your CTL? Y / N
- Do they align with the role of your CTL as previously described?   Y / N
- Are they clear and clearly applicable to what you do? Y / N
- Are they visible to you and the campus community?   Y / N

Value Statement

Vision and mission statements are an integral part of any organization's strategic plan, but not all strategic plans contain value statements. Values are the overarching principles that define who we are as humans in this profession. They connect us to our mission, to our campus, and to ourselves. Often, this reflects the bonds we build, the relationships we foster, the outreach we do, the dedication we have to our faculty, our field, our students, our university, and our craft. If you want to include a value statement in your strategic plan, it might be helpful to start with the values of our field as they are articulated by a leading professional society, the POD Network (Figure 5.2).

While (hopefully) the meaning of most of these is self-evident, there are two values worthy of further comment. The first is respect and ethical practices, which are further articulated in the statement on ethical guidelines (POD Network, n.d.). Among other standards, these guidelines emphasize the distinctive cloak of confidentiality that envelopes our work, a standard that can require practice and experience to navigate appropriately.

66   TAKING FLIGHT

WORKSHEET 5.1
Means, Ends, and Evidence

Mission Statement Goals	Strategies	Evidence of Success
What we will do	How we will do it	How we will measure it

Figure 5.2. The POD Network value statement

The Professional and Organizational Development Network in Higher Education values and is committed to…

1. Collegiality
2. Inclusion
3. Diverse perspectives
4. Advocacy and Social justice
5. Distributed Leadership
6. Innovation
7. Evidence-Based Practices
8. Respect/Ethical Practices

(Source: https://podnetwork.org/about-us/mission/)

Figure 5.3. Pulling it all together: An example of CTL vision, mission, goals, and values.

Mission, Vision & Values

The mission of The Teaching Center is to inspire excellence and innovation in teaching, learning, and scholarly activities at the University of Pittsburgh. The University Center for Teaching and Learning endeavors to achieve this mission by:

- Providing expertise in instructional design and development
- Developing and supporting teaching and learning environments
- Effectively applying current and emerging instructional technologies
- Delivering services for the assessment, measurement, and evaluation of teaching
- Collaborating with University partners and external colleagues
- Delivering professional creative and production services for University events and activities
- Providing superior service to the University community

Figure 5.3. (*Continued*)

	The Teaching Center will be nationally and internationally recognized as a model resource center for teaching, learning, and technology in higher education. Because we are integral to the success of the University of Pittsburgh, we: • are leaders in the innovative use of scholarly research in teaching and learning • are leaders in the innovative use of technology in support of teaching, learning, and scholarly activities • incorporate learning research and best practices in faculty development that promote quality course design and the effective integration of technology in teaching and learning • provide high-quality, mission-critical services to the University
	Our work is guided by these values, and we are committed to: • *Excellence* in all we do • *Collaboration* within and beyond the University • *Innovation* to find and apply best practices • *Service* to the University community

These guidelines can also serve as an effective teaching tool when you are acculturating a new colleague or faculty fellow into the work of your CTL. The second value is diverse perspectives; it serves as a reminder to us to be mindful of the splendid variety of ways to teach, to learn, and/or to develop effectively.

Step 4: Being a Pillar of Support

CTLs need to be mindful of more than their own mission and values. They should also be mindful of, even driven by, the role they play in advancing the university mission and culture. In "Establishing an Educational Development

Program," Douglas L. Robertson (2010) poses a question many of us take for granted: "Should there be a center?" (p. 37). Of course we answer *yes*, but let's shift the conversation from why *we* think there should be a center to if and why *others* believe there should be a CTL.

And this is a question we should always be asking ourselves. There is a very real danger of revolving-door cynicism, for example, the mind-set that administrators, programs, strategic plans, and "the next big thing" and "who we are" branding come and go, but we'll still be here. We simply cannot afford to believe that because our center was created, we're set. Rather, it is incumbent on us to routinely reaffirm our role in the advancement of the university knowing—believe it or not—that there are detractors and competitors, as well as shifting sands of administrative support, priorities, and even whims. We should strive, individually and as a unit, to be ahead of the curve and at the drop of a hat and in every aspect of our programming be able to demonstrate our alignment with, integration into, and (hopefully) even leadership of institutional initiatives.

The starting point for such conversations invariably involves the university's strategic plan, QEP (Quality Enhancement Plan), or other such instrument that conveys the official institutional mission (C. Sweet & Blythe, 2010). It may also apply to more ethereal concepts, such as what it means to be a land-grant university, to have a service mission, or other uniquely identifiable aspects of your institution's identity (Tassoni, 2010). In a simple world it's a matching game, drawing lines between the university's plan and your own. This is actually a sound and frequently exercised strategy: Find the pillar of the plan that matches your CTL's mission and argue in your strategic plan how your center is essential to it. Once these lines are drawn, draw new lines connecting your services to other aspects of the plan and conclude with a compelling description of how everything you do is woven into the tapestry of the university's mission.

Worksheet 5.2 is designed to facilitate this process by providing a framework for linking your mission to your university's goals. It helps us when we are deep into the detailed aspects of our plans while keeping an eye on the big picture. When complete, it provides you with something around which you can organize your programming as well as a clear articulation of your center's commitment to, and role in, promoting the institutional mission.

Although these 1:1 relationships serve a clear administrative purpose, it is possible—and strategically wise—to assess, understand, and identify the degree to which we contribute to the larger vision and mission of the university. We routinely want to push ourselves to think bigger, develop a clear measure of where we are, where we want to be, and how we can accomplish

WORKSHEET 5.2
Supporting the Strategic Plan

Pillar 1	How We Support It	Pillar 2	How We Support It	Pillar 3	How We Support It	Overall Mission	How We Support It
1a		2a		3a			
1b		2b		3b			
1c		2c		3c			
1d		2d		3d			

those goals within the context of our institutions. It can be beneficial in a myriad of ways to understand and articulate the degree to which we are aligned with, integrated into, or serve as an agent of change on your campus.

Imagine a complexity continuum ranging from least complex (aligned) to moderately complex (integrated) to highly complex (a driver of institutional change) (Figure 5.4).

First, and in general, are you mostly *aligned with*, *integrated into*, or a *driver of* campus culture?

Now think about your university mission statement, strategic plan, QEP, and so on.

Figure 5.4. Alignment, integration, or a driver?

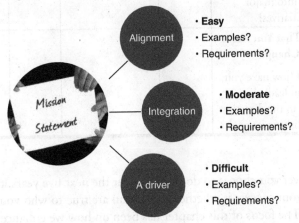

Here are some examples to guide your thinking. If your institution's strategic plan calls for technology-enhanced learning, and part of your mission is to support faculty in their efforts to use educational technology in the classroom, then it is likely your efforts are integrated with others on campus, such as IT or distance education, who support different facets of the same goal. If your accrediting body has questioned your institution's reliance on student evaluations of instruction as the sole measure of teaching effectiveness, your CTL may consider whether to act as a driver and lead an initiative that supports the adoption of teaching portfolios, knowing that there are considerable obstacles in your path. If your campus is applying for "engaged" status with Carnegie, you might want to be aligned with that aspiration by partnering with your office of community engagement to provide programming related to course design and service-learning, and perhaps consider expanding such programming in the future.

TABLE 5.1

	Doing	Can/Should Do	How	Obstacles?
Evidence of Institutional Alignment Where and how are you aligned with/how do you support the vision and mission of the institution?				
Evidence of Integration Where and how well is your CTL established/ integrated into major campus initiatives?				
Evidence That You Are a Driver of Change Where and how have you led (can you lead) the institution in the direction of accomplishing its goals?				

Whatever you choose to do, now or over the next five years, the primary marker of your success is whether or not you are true to who you are—your hedgehog. The focus of this chapter has been on how we enhance the awareness of ourselves and direct that toward significant goals. We definitely do not want to be eaten by the fox. Nor do we want to become the fox. One of the challenges you will likely face in your role is shifting thinking from service to leadership. It is not necessarily a trade-off: We do provide services to faculty and the campus community, but we can—indeed, must—leverage our experience and knowledge to assert and earn a leadership identity. And there are no self-fulfilling prophecies at work here—saying we're agents of change does not make it so; rather, we get there through strategic collaboration, alignment, and integration. Accordingly, a desirable place to land should focus less on location than on the idea of educational development itself—to inform practice, to advance individual and institutional success, and to provide a space—physical, virtual, intellectual, and discursive—to imagine, explore, and collaborate on strategies to promote the cause of teaching and learning in higher education.

6

PRIORITIZATION

What Will You Do First?

Attending your first national or international educational development conference has some parallels to planning the programming for your center. Surrounded by an engaged community of faculty developers, you begin the conference with unbridled enthusiasm. People here are as passionate as you are about advocating for high-quality teaching and learning. For a few short days you will be preaching to the choir. This is going to be rejuvenating, educational, and fun. You enthusiastically peruse the program until you realize there are several innovative interactive sessions that interest you at every time slot. How will you choose just one session, potentially missing something that would revolutionize programming for your CTL? Should you run from workshop plan A to plan B if the first does not immediately look useful? Attend the one that your colleagues are going to? Attend the ones your colleagues are not going to? Toss a coin or attempt to cover all the bases by settling for a roundtable where you will leave with a myriad of tried-and-tested options? How do you decide what is the absolute best investment of time at this conference in support of your CTL's mission? By the third day of the conference, fatigue and despair set in. You have been to fantastic sessions led by experts in this field where you have explored what really works to improve teaching and student success. For you, implementing even half of these innovations into center programming would be like climbing Mount Everest with no oxygen—a near impossible task.

This is an analogy for the choices you face when deciding how best to prioritize regardless of whether you are new to the role or reflecting on your past year's successes. You want to plan and deliver the absolute best programming for your campus, but which evidence-based teaching and learning techniques should you focus on? Should you focus on supporting early or midcareer

73

faculty? Should you prioritize support for a popular national initiative or one aspect of teaching that your provost wants to see addressed on campus? To add to this complex set of decisions, when you have decided what the focus should be, which methods for delivering programs to faculty, staff, or students are you going to use and which will be the most effective?

To further complicate identifying strategic priorities, educational developers often take on center leadership with little to no experience beyond being recognized for teaching or service excellence (Chism, Gosling, & Sorcinelli, 2010; Green & Little, 2016) and may not be a full-time director. Someone taking on a new center may be attempting to juggle prioritization of programming with activities like increasing visibility and reputation (Siering et al., 2015). Regardless of your baseline, institutional context, or the resources you have at your disposal, whether learning at a large conference or delving into the literature, you are guaranteed to be overwhelmed with many more opportunities for educational innovation than you can include in your current portfolio of program offerings, particularly if your time or resources are limited. If this describes you, the good news is that you are not on your own. There is a large evidence-based and highly collaborative community waiting to help you prioritize.

This chapter will guide you through a full consideration of your stakeholders on campus who have a vested interest in the success of your center along with the methods for delivering faculty development programming that has been proven most impactful at every career stage. By the end of this chapter, you will have the components of a one-, three-, or five-year plan of strategic priorities for programing accounting for the time and resources you have available.

Your Mission . . . Should You Choose to Accept It

Whether you have to turn around an ineffective center, are undergoing a major structural reorganization, or are just evaluating your next strategic plan, prioritizing your programming will help you achieve quality faculty development. Identifying center priorities can be challenging. Success breeds success, so if your CTL has a good reputation for achieving cultural change on campus, different units may instigate a "tug-of-war" over your involvement in their agendas. This can create opportunities for productive collaborative work with separate units on campus or it can lead to mission creep, which can negatively impact the effectiveness and reputation of your center, if not fully aligned with the purpose of the CTL (Siering et al.,

2015). What you decide to prioritize must reflect your institutional vision, mission, strategic plan, and be matched appropriately by your available time and resources.

Balancing priorities is a genuine challenge because faculty are not the only ones who benefit from effective development. Staff may also participate, while students have a vested interest in quality teaching and learning during their educational journey. Administrators may look to you to justify resource allocation to your center or to help make their new initiative succeed. Your marketing or recruiting offices may feature your programming as an example of the excellent education your institution is offering to students. Because of this, serving as a CTL director is one of the jobs on any campus that—when done well—has the potential to positively impact everyone.

Spending time and resources promoting excellence in teaching and learning makes sense from the faculty viewpoint, but there are many other stakeholders in the success of your center: students, faculty, staff, administrators, and maybe even politicians. When developing your CTL strategic priorities, you will need to think about how you frame other people's priorities as your own (Bolman & Gallos, 2010), whether supporting your dean's favorite initiative for political capital or taking into account the preferences of influential faculty. CTL directors walk a tightrope between faculty and administration; teaching to remain relevant while at the same time building productive working relationships with staff across campus and upper level administrators even when that relationship shifts with a different vision or mandate (Sorcinelli, 2002). You identified the people on your campus who have a stake in your center in chapter 5; now we will explore strategies for building on that information to determine on which programs, projects, and initiatives you will want to focus your efforts.

Taking Flight Scenario
The following people come into your office at the same time:

- The provost, who has what she says is a quick question about teaching evaluations
- An agitated faculty member who wants to talk about a sensitive issue regarding something that just happened in her classroom
- A student from one of your classes who wants to talk about the next assignment
- A staff member who needs your input/review on a report that is due later the same day

Continues

Taking Flight Scenario (*Continued*)

> - Your administrative assistant, who needs you to sign three forms today or funds will be denied
> - The dean of the College of Business who wants to talk to you about a faculty member who is really struggling with their teaching
> - The head of the office of institutional assessment, who says that they need time to talk to you as soon as possible about a new assessment of teaching and learning
> - The director of service–learning, with whom you are currently working on a big project, who wants to plan an event that takes place the following week
> - A colleague who says they have a really great idea for a new SoTL project
> - Your partner/significant other, who wants to take you out for a surprise lunch
>
> Who do you serve first? In what order do you handle the others? What do you tell them? Why did you choose the order that you did?[1]

In addition to considering your stakeholder groups, teaching is a highly personal endeavor. What works for one does not necessarily work for another, and faculty have different development needs at different stages of their career (Austin, Sorcinelli, & McDaniels, 2007; Gardner, 2005). Educational development is a young discipline, but despite the myriad of considerations, strategies and approaches that you can use to prioritize programming, we have a pretty good idea about what specific types of programs are highly effective (Beach, Sorcinelli, Austin, & Rivard, 2016). Whether your mandate is to focus on building several programs at a time or scaling back to focus on one impactful evidence-based technique for a larger audience, someone before you has tried it and written about how it went.

The worksheets that follow will guide you through our Taking Flight stages to help you define which considerations are most important for you in prioritizing your programming, as well as facilitate an exploration of different strategies you can use to form your strategic priorities. The exercises provide reflective questions to facilitate a review and identification of your top priorities along with practical planning tools in assessing these considerations within your institutional context. You will then have the opportunity to consider how you will maximize your time and resources and begin to build these priorities into a step-by-step framework for a one-, three-, or five- strategic plan. Your mission is to carefully balance the needs of the stakeholders as you decide and build on existing priorities for your CTL. Remember, Rome was not built in a day. What will you do first?

Taking Flight—One Stage at a Time

Whatever focus for your programming and delivery method you choose, the good news is that there is strong evidence that participation in faculty development programming, whether formal or informal, does positively impact student learning (Condon, Iverson, Manduca, & Rutz, 2016). Those impacts are pervasive over a career through discussions and sharing of materials among colleagues (M. Wright, Horii, Felten, Sorcinelli, & Kaplan, 2018). Therefore, regardless of your center structure, quality programming can help advance the teaching and learning culture on your campus (Cook & Kaplan, 2011).

We will work through our Taking Flight stages to identify your priorities: from building your nest in Stage 1 by gathering the information from your needs analysis through learning to fly by considering priorities from the angle of each set of stakeholders and setting goals in Stage 2. We will then soar high by working through a planning exercise to maximize your time and resources in Stage 3, then return home in Stage 4 by reflecting on what is currently working and what needs renewal.

Stage 1: Building Your Nest: Do Your Homework

Commonly referred to as the input or listening phase of any new campus leadership project, in this stage, you solicit clear expectations from faculty and other stakeholders on programs they would like to see running or timely and effective feedback on your existing programs (see chapter 3). When designing a variety of programs to meet this shared vision there are several critical components to include regardless of your priorities. This would usually mean do your homework, but we have already done that with you. Bring the results of your baseline assessment (chapter 2), your needs analysis (chapter 3), and a preliminary list of your mission and strategic goals (chapter 5), so that you can be specific as we work through these worksheets.

Stage 2: Learning to Fly: Setting Goals

Just as developers show faculty how to set learning outcomes for their courses, setting performance outcomes for your programming facilitates planning and assessment, and it is sometimes stronger to have a consistent theme for a number of years rather than a mosaic of offerings. If faculty can articulate exactly what your CTL provides in terms of services, that is good evidence that you have both prioritized and communicated your strengths appropriately (Shahid, 2012).

You can start by situating your process within the vision, mission, and cultural values of your institution, your CTL, and the campus teaching and learning community. Looking at your work through this lens entails considerations of meaning and significance and how you model, reflect, and shape the implicit and explicit ethos and narratives of your university. For example, many CTLs followed-up on recent tragedies by developing programming specifically aimed to support faculty as they navigated conversations and repercussions of these events with their students. By doing so, they reinforced the norms of their community and strengthened a sense of belonging.

Ask Yourself:

- Are there aspects of your institutional mission that indicate specific programming should be a priority?
- Are there timely issues or challenges on campus that you could address with your programming?
- Are there specific programs that reflect who you are as an institution and what is important to your faculty, staff, and students?
- Are there specific programs that reflect what you want to be known for as a CTL? What programs contribute the most to telling your story?

You may also wish to consider departmental, institutional, university system, and/or national initiatives with which you can align programming with a particular emphasis on the distribution of resources and how you can best compete to get your fair share of them.

Ask Yourself:

- What are your supervisor's priorities and how could your programming support those?
- What are the primary issues being considered in your faculty governance bodies (e.g., senate) and how could your programming address those?
- What national, regional, or statewide initiatives might be applicable to your institutional context?
- Are there topics-based multi-institutional initiatives with which you would like to align (e.g., AAC&U High-Impact Practices, Complete College America, Gardiner Institute Gateways to Completion Project)?
- Are there local community or industry stakeholders that could build political capital for your CTL?

You might also want to take into consideration the people who make up your CTL, whether it is your staff, your constituents, or even yourself. In terms of your primary constituents, faculty, our field has recently begun working to integrate the faculty life-cycle, for example, the idea that faculty have different needs in educational development at different stages of their career and that meeting those needs involves different kinds of programming.

- *Early Career*—focus on enhancing skill in the classroom with new faculty orientation to the institution and/or teaching depending on the group, workshops on different aspects of teaching
- *Midcareer*—focus on career assessment, leadership development, sabbaticals, and so on
- *Late Career*—focus on mentoring of younger colleagues, institutional service

Ask Yourself:

- What balance of faculty do you have? What types of faculty development do they need?
- Does your CTL want to focus on new-career, midcareer, or late-career faculty first or balance the needs of faculty at all career stages?
- Can you identify any gaps in your support for a particular life-cycle cohort?

A final consideration is the logistics of programming, such as how you will deliver your programming; how/how often/when you will provide programming; how you will manage your events; and how you will address potential logistical obstacles, such as a lack of shared university calendars, printing restrictions, privacy concerns (for recorded sessions), technological limitations (such as no Wi-Fi or projectors), or difficult class schedules around which your programs must be scheduled.

Ask Yourself:

- How will you determine when, where, and how you will hold your events and programs?
- Who will have oversight for planning and managing your events and programs (keeping in mind that these may be two different people)?
- How will you handle routine program functions, such as registration, name tags, sign-in sheets, evaluation forms, swag/giveaways, handouts, technical support, publicity, catering, and time keeping?
- What kinds of resources (financial and human) do you have available to support your programs?
- What are the biggest logistical obstacles for programming on your campus and how do you plan to address these?

In addition to analyzing your programs from these perspectives, you might also want to consider your own interests. What can you be passionate about when it comes to teaching, learning, and/or faculty development? Are you interested in increasing opportunities for undergraduate research or experiential learning? Are you interested in supporting the development of a positive academic mind-set in your students? Or maybe you are a fan of the positive impact of collaborative or team-based learning? Whatever your passion is, you are likely to be more successful when advocating for things that you yourself are interested in and knowledgeable about. This is a perfectly valid aspect to consider as you prioritize. We all want to encourage the advancement of evidence-based practice in areas we care about and that does not happen by accident.

Stage 3: Soaring High: Building Your Programs

When choosing what to build on to take your center to the next level, taking time to assess which programs will help your faculty achieve the goals you have set out for your center is preferable to simply following what works in other contexts. Tailoring programs to your specific needs earns your center the respect of both faculty and administrators. Considering which programs are right for you and which are the highest priorities if your budget is limited will help your center soar to the appropriate and sustainable height.

Which Programs Are Right for You?

You should now have a pretty good idea of what you want (or need) the goals of your programming to be. That leads us to the next question: What kinds of programs should you offer? We would love to be able to tell you that there is a magic list of faculty development programs that you should offer, and all you have to do is copy these down and implement them. There are a number of long-standing and widely used programming modalities, such as faculty learning communities, for which a considerable body of research has developed to support them. There are also a number of long-standing and widely used programming modalities, such as the workshop, for which a considerable body of research has developed that does not support them. There are also a number of programming modalities that are either too new or too limited in their application to have received research attention (at least not yet). A recent study revealed that the most popular modalities for CTLs were "one to three" hour workshops, consultations, and web resources, but in the same study, none of these were rated (by the same people who offered them) as most effective (Chism, 2012). What this means is that your guiding principle shouldn't be just the quantity of evidence, the examples of others, the test of time, or even the popular vote. Rather, you should look at what kinds of programs will work with your faculty to help you achieve the goals of your CTL.

The workshop is an especially beleaguered example of this. An increasing body of evidence suggests that one-off or one-and-done workshops on a given topic are pretty ineffective, regardless of how well they are done. This is true especially if you consider long-term retention and application (Henderson, Beach, & Finkelstein, 2011). We may know this, but our faculty may not. If they are expecting one-off, stand-alone workshops, then they can be resistant when you try to vary your programming. The nature of this pushback is not dissimilar to student resistance to new forms of teaching; we tend to be most comfortable with what we are familiar with, and what we believe works based on that experience. If your faculty are expecting workshops and you don't give them workshops, you run the danger of being seen as unresponsive, ineffective, or resistant yourself. In this case, it can be helpful to view workshops as a gateway, or first step, toward programming with more lasting impact or programming that simply lasts longer. Long-running sustained programs, such as 60-plus hours over 4 to 18 months, year-long institutes, or academies have been shown to make a demonstrable impact on teaching practice, especially when compared to stand-alone workshops (Condon et al., 2016). Such programs may produce more depth, but they struggle with breadth, as they are often, by their nature, confined to small cohorts of faculty who are able to invest the time. Peer observations of teaching and small-group analysis (both methods for getting feedback about how students learn in your classroom) have been shown to have a major impact on teaching practice, especially when coupled with pre- and postconsultations (Donnelly, 2007; Felten, Little, & Pingree, 2004), but these can be time-consuming for you and challenging to scale. These kinds of feedback activities, too, can be sensitive to campus culture, especially the levels of mutual trust, making them not always the best choice as a showcase program for a new CTL. Faculty learning communities have a proven track record as a low-cost, high-impact means for extending your reach, but they have to be managed well to achieve their desired goals, and that takes time, effort, and training (for facilitators).

Which Programs Are Your Highest Priority?

Now that you've gathered your input, set your goals, and become familiar with the pros and cons of some common programming elements, you're ready to start choosing the programs that are right for you. Using Table 6.1, for each programming modality, indicate the amount to which they are a priority across the different prioritization categories (e.g., resources, mission). The exercise uses a 5-point scale with 5 indicating your highest priority. For example, workshops on teaching techniques might rate a 3 for vision (not directly student learning), a 2 for resources (low return on investment [ROI]), a four for faculty (popular), and a three on student classroom needs (technology use is higher priority). Do not worry about the total number of top priorities at this stage because we will do a step-by-step comparison in the next section.

Once you have completed the first part of the exercise, take your top seven priorities and fill in the row and column headings in Table 6.2. For example, if an annual conference had the highest value then put that in cell AA. Then compare each of your top seven priorities, side-by-side, systematically using the following paired comparison analysis tool.

To do the paired comparison, put the letter in the box that represents the top two priorities within each comparison, and add a relative importance score out of five over the other option where five is the highest and one is the lowest. For example, in comparing the relative importance of your annual conference (A) to peer consultations (B) in the starred box would be A4 for Dalton State College. This will help you rank your top priorities. Total the

TABLE 6.1

Determining Your Programming Priorities

	Vision, Mission or Mandate	Available Resources	Faculty Need	Student Classroom Needs	Total
Institutional Priorities: Faculty Development Programming					
1. Workshops on Teaching Techniques					
2. Workshops on Instructional Technologies					
3. Faculty Recognition Programs (TAP)					
4. Classroom Observations & Personal Consultations					
5. New Faculty Orientation					
6. Faculty Learning Communities					
7. Annual Teaching and Learning Conference					
8. Showcase of Student or Faculty Scholarship					
9. Faculty Fellows Programs					
10. Informal Communities Based Around Common Interest					

(Continues)

TABLE 6.1 *(CONTINUED)*

	Vision, Mission or Mandate	Available Resources	Faculty Need	Student Classroom Needs	Total
11.	Scholarship of Teaching & Learning Support					
12.	Leadership Development					
13.	Course Redesign or Other Initiatives					
14.	Grant Writing					
15.	Peer Mentoring Programs					
16.	Social Community Building Events, (e.g., coffee and conversation about teaching and learning)					
17.	Center Publications (e.g., blog, journal, newsletter)					
18.	One to Three Day Academies/Retreats					

Indicate the seven priorities with the highest total above......

TABLE 6.2
Paired Comparison Matrix: Programming Priorities

Option	A.	B.	C.	D.	E.	F.	G.
A.		*					
B.							
C.							
D.							
E.							
F.							
G.							

number for each letter to identify your overall ranked priorities. List them in order below the matrix.

> *Ask yourself:*
>
> What are your top priorities after this exercise?

Which Programs Can You Actually Do?

There are always more bright ideas and exciting opportunities than available time and many of us have more on our "wish lists" than we have time or money to do. This next exercise prompts you to analyze what might be a quick win and what might take a lot of effort without bringing significant reward and/or take too many resources (time, energy, or money). In addition, regardless of your plans, spending time securing and justifying your use of financial and human resources for programming has to be a priority. In a time where value for money is a common conversation in academia, it is no different in teaching and learning. In Figure 6.2, we turn a global view of what is possible into something you can actually do.

> *Taking Flight* Scenario
> Imagine that you have a choice to engage you and your CTL in the following projects, all of which should last for at least one academic year. You may choose as many—or as few—as you think you can handle.
>
> - Leading a campus-wide initiative to integrate ePortfolios
> - Being a member of a steering committee to establish GradesFirst, which tracks student success metrics and facilitates advising
> - Serving on a committee to support digital humanities efforts across campus
> - Initiating a new program to showcase the work of campus-wide teaching award winners
> - Cofacilitating a one-credit course for undergraduate students who will serve as partners in SoTL projects
> - Developing a workshop on how to put together a tenure portfolio
> - Consulting with the QEP/accreditation director to develop new avenues for educating faculty on QEP outcomes
> - Serving on a task force to determine campus compliance with new accessibility requirements

(Continues)

Taking Flight Scenario (Continued)

> - Working with a collaborative group of researchers to publish a SoTL article based on a recent institutional initiative
> - Establishing an open classroom project
>
> Which of these would you choose? What criteria do you use to help determine your choices?

Ask Yourself:

> - How much of your time can you devote to programming efforts?
> - How much staff support do you have? How much time can they devote to programming efforts?
> - Who else can provide additional programming support?
> - What is your all-in programming budget?

As much as we might like to, we can't be all things to all people, so we have to choose.

The following list describes some common criteria used to determine programming feasibility.

Your Time. It is highly unlikely that running programs is all that you are expected to do. At a minimum, a recent international study showed that 95% of us maintain teaching responsibilities in addition to our educational development work; 80% of us maintain a scholarly agenda, whether in SoTL or our discipline (Green & Little, 2016); and many of us devote additional time to university and community service. While these activities can help with our currency, credibility, and community, it means that we often risk being stretched very thin. It can be more effective to do fewer programs very well than to try to stretch too far and do more programs but at lower levels of effectiveness.

Your Supporting Staff. It can be very helpful to take into consideration the strength of your team, as well as your individual strengths and what you each contribute to the programming efforts. If you are looking to hire a team, consider finding a balance of strengths and weaknesses. For example, perhaps you enjoy the logistical details that go into planning events, but you find it challenging to tell your story; hire a symbolic thinker with graphic design skills. You could also look for opportunities to delegate work to part-time workers, volunteers, interns, student workers, faculty fellows, close friends, responsible offspring, or other supporting players who may or may not be on the official payroll (see chapter 4 for more discussion about staffing).

Scalability. One way to leverage your existing resources is to consider ways to scale your programs so that they no longer need you to be directly involved. In this train-the-trainer model, you train and empower faculty, staff, or students to deliver programming to others. You might say that this is the educational development equivalent of bacterial growth, and it can quickly grow in new petri dishes across campus. By using faculty fellows or academy graduates as proto educational developers, you get the added benefits of providing peer models and increasing your visibility while at also the same time extending the faculty member's CV and/or annual evaluation reports.

Your Budget. It is pretty easy to underestimate how much programs will cost if you don't have much experience in running them. You may have a sense of the major costs, such as facilitator fees or food, but have you thought about the cost of copies, photographers, space, permits, parking, or all of the other little expenses that can add up? We recommend rounding up, and then being pleasantly surprised if you have funds remaining.

Ask Yourself:

- What types of faculty development can you reasonably accommodate on your current budget?
- Is your current budget sufficient to serve your mission or do you need to advocate for more?
- What impact will you have with your current programming budget?
- What impact could you have if your programming budget were increased?

ROI. What all of the prior criteria add up to is your ROI. This is a calculation of how much benefit you will get from a particular program, whether that benefit comes in the form of reputation, resources, relationships, or processes, versus how much time, energy, and resources it will take to do it. This calculation can be used both to determine which programs you will offer and which programs you will decommission (Brinthaupt, Cruz, Otto, & Pinter, 2019).

WORKSHEET 6.1
Investment of Resources Diagram.

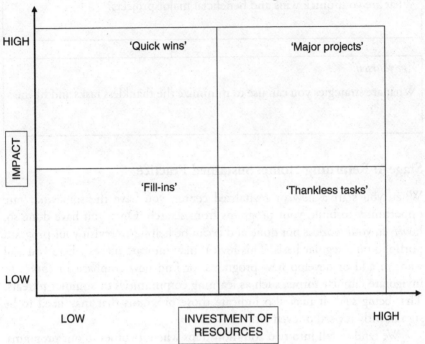

We can now use that ROI calculation to rank your priorities in an action matrix (Worksheet 6.1). For this exercise, we will be arranging your potential programs into one of the following four categories:

1. Quick wins: Tasks that do not require a high level of time or resources, but are high impact.
2. Major projects: These involve a large investment of time and money but with high impact.
3. Fill-ins: Periodic programs done on an as-needed basis, often low expenditure but also low impact.
4. Thankless tasks: These require a high input of time and money but are often low or indirect impact.

This analysis enables you to balance your ROI, but it can also serve as a reminder to try to tip the balance of your activities toward the more productive quadrants. In this way, you can keep yourselves moving forward.

> *Ask Yourself:*
>
> What are your quick wins and beneficial major projects?

> *Ask yourself:*
>
> What are strategies you can use to minimize the thankless tasks and fill-ins?

Stage 4: Returning Home: Sustained Practice

When you start a new or revitalized center, you have the somewhat rare opportunity to build your programs from scratch. Once you have done so, however, your work is not done and it can be helpful to revisit your program portfolio on a regular basis. This review may indicate places where you will want to add or develop new programs, or find new emphasis or topics to invigorate familiar forms, such as learning communities or summer retreats. That being said, it may also indicate those programs that may need to be significantly revised or even retired.

We tend to fall into two common traps when it comes to our programs. The first, called a rigidity trap, is when we have trouble letting go of long-standing programs that have become part of our identity or legacy. For example, it can be difficult to discontinue the summer institute you've been offering for the past 20 years because you have faculty supporters who take it as a point of pride that they've attended every one. Or perhaps you have a team member who takes particular pride in their responsibility for a program that is no longer thriving. For these reasons, the challenge surrounding creative destruction is often in strengthening, rather than weakening, these interpersonal relationships.

The poverty trap occurs when we maintain programs, largely on life support, providing sufficient resources to keep them operational, but not really enough to make them thrive. This could be a program left over from your predecessor, perhaps, that has some participants but that you aren't terribly interested growing, or perhaps it's something you'd like to grow, but you've lost some of the funding or support staff to sustain it. Or, perhaps someone suggested a great program and you had a hard time saying no to them. For all of these occasions, the decision comes down to whether you're willing to commit to giving it the support it needs (perhaps even taking support away

Figure 6.1. CTL program life cycle analysis.

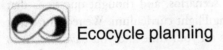

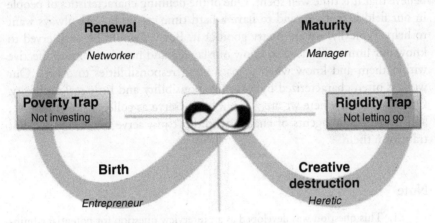

Source: http://liberatingstructures.com/33-ecocycle—planning/ (Creative Commons license).

Use the **life cycle analysis** tool to analyze the life left in your current programming within the center or within the campus. This can help you identify projects that have been awarded funding that may not be providing an ROI and could be creatively destroyed to provide increased resources for other programs. Alternatively, there may be new projects that have been a priority for a while but are caught in a poverty trap.

from other programs to do so), or whether it is time to cut or significantly rethink how you will continue to serve that need.

You may find that your CTL, too, goes through a life cycle. Indeed, this is the basis of the Taking Flight model. Rather than letting fear or complacency take you into either a poverty or rigidity trap, we encourage you to embrace the inherently dynamic nature of the close relationship between a CTL and the campus community it serves. In the end, these are not really our programs; they belong to everyone, and we should be grateful that we get to serve as their stewards. And gratitude is not a bad principle to apply across all of your programming. We recommend that you exude gratitude to faculty for taking the time to participate in your events and programs. Thank them for the work they do; provide them with a visible reminder of that gratitude, whether in the form of certificates of completion or handwritten thank-you cards for those who go above and beyond.

Speaking of gratitude, we are very appreciative that you are taking the time to work through the exercises, scenarios, and thought questions that we have provided as part of our Taking Flight curriculum. We recognize that you have a large number of demands on your time and you have chosen to spend your time with us over these competing priorities. That being said, we believe that it is time well spent. One of the defining characteristics of people in our field is that we tend to have a hard time saying no. We always want to help. Typically, we are pretty good at it. But we would be well served to know our limits. We need to know our lane(s) and how to be most effective within them and know when to pass along responsibilities to others. Our work is often characterized by lots of responsibility and little real authority. Once we accept where we are, we can better serve as collegial, collaborative, and instrumental agents of change who don't just serve our campuses, but transform them.

Note

1. This question was developed as an interview question for potential administrative assistants for a new CTL. The responses proved to be illuminating.

7

COMMUNICATION

How Will You Tell Your Story?

In his famous book *The 7 Habits of Highly Effective People*, Stephen Covey's (2004) principle of interpersonal communication is summed up in the phrase "first seek to understand, then to be understood" (p. 235). The basis of this habit, according to Covey, is an emphasis on empathic listening, which means that you "listen with the intent to understand, not with the intent to reply" (p. 235). The adage is deceptively simple and often proves to be considerably more difficult to adhere to during real-life situations. History is full of examples of what happens when this principle is not followed, the outcomes of which are sometimes funny, embarrassing, or even tragic, all of which you may have already experienced because empathic listening is at the heart of our consultation work; and it takes some practice to master. As you continue to practice, take heart in the fact that you have already taken the time to listen to your campus through the needs assessment process. Now, it's time to turn that insight into the basis of how you want to be understood. Let's talk about how you're going to communicate who you are, what you do, why you do it, and why it matters.

Communication Function 1: Getting the Word Out (Marketing and Branding)

If you don't have a background in marketing (or similar fields), the prospect of developing some parts of your communication plan may seem especially daunting. We've all been there. From what we've experienced, the secret to success is to break down the task of communication into manageable components and then build those components up over time, not unlike stacking up blocks to make a tower. At the most basic level, communication is about letting people know who you are and what you do. What this means is that the baseline of your communication strategy will focus on creating a handful of integrated tools, some old and some new, that will enable you to market you and your services (McKendree, 2012). While there are multiple channels by which you can get the word out (and those seem to be expanding exponentially every day), Table 7.1 lists some of the most common communication tools that CTLs develop for themselves.

TABLE 7.1
Common CTL Communication Outlets

Print	Digital	Other
Flyers	CTL website	CTL logo/tag line
Guides or visual references	Press releases	Pins or buttons
Brochures	CTL social media (e.g. Twitter, Facebook; LinkedIn)	Clothing items (e.g., T-shirts, hats)
Formal Reports (often annual or quarterly)	Newsletters	Branded swag (e.g., calendars, umbrellas, clocks, flash drives)
Business or contact cards	Listservs/Email subscription groups	Pens, pencils, other office items

---

Taking Flight Tip

A recent development in CTL marketing, the "call-me" card, shown close to real size in Figure 7.1, serves as a kind of super business card for your center, as in the first example, or for an individual, as in the second. The gist of a call-me card is that you tell the holder when they should call you. For a CTL, it can distinguish staff roles, and for an individual, it can act as an incentive to potential constituents.

Ask Yourself:

- What is your hedgehog? What are your center's strengths, vision, and mission? See chapters 5 and 6 for more ideas on how to develop these.
- Who needs to know who you are and what you do? In other words, who is your audience, or, perhaps better stated, who are your audiences?
- Why and when do you want people to seek you out?
- What distinguishes what you do from what other units on campus do? Other CTLs? Other universities?

Figure 7.1. Call-me cards (CTL and individual) front and back views.

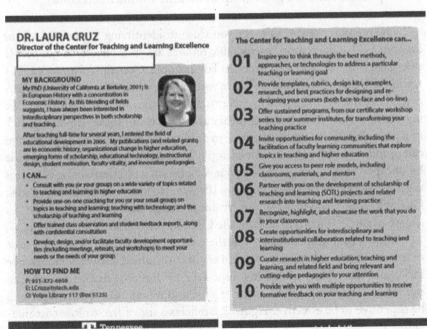

Note: The specific details are not sharply rendered intentionally, as these may change over time.

Having the means to get your message out will not help you if you don't have a sense of what you would like that message to be and who you think should hear it. This is the basis of your *brand*.

There are a large number of branding exercises you and your team can do together in order to develop your marketing focus; the following list shows just a few short examples. A good brand takes some time to develop, so don't be frustrated if you don't get to a final product right away. Consider the following examples:

- *Branding Exercise 1:* The Comparison Game. If your CTL were a car, what kind of car would it be and why? You can substitute all kinds of categories for the word *car*; for example, What kind of food? What famous novel or movie?
- *Branding Exercise 2:* The Windfall. A wealthy and anonymous benefactor wants to give your CTL $1 million to spend on one (and only one) program, activity, or initiative that will have the most impact on your strategic goals. What would you spend it on?
- *Branding Exercise 3:* The Six-Word Memoir. Write the story of your CTL using only six words—no more, no less. This is harder than it sounds, and you might want to reference the six-word memoir phenomenon as a guide (https://www.sixwordmemoirs.com/).

The memoir exercise may get you close to identifying a potential *tagline* for your CTL. These short, memorable phrases are your "hook" to get people to engage with you and your services. For example, Cornell University's CTL's tagline "Give us five minutes we'll save you an hour" dramatically increased participation from busy faculty who were attracted to the promise of efficiency. We know a few tricks from learning theory about what can make something stick in a person's brain, so do not hesitate to apply these to your own message. You can introduce a tipping point, for example, by making your message just a little bit unexpected. You can also make your message stick by intertwining two ideas together in a novel or interesting way (Brown, Roediger, & McDaniel, 2014; Gladwell, 2006). You may want to try out potential taglines on guinea pigs . . . uh, we mean . . . friends or allies of the CTL, as your informal focus group.

So, you have your message and the tools to disseminate it; now it's time to activate your marketing plan. In an era of constrained resources, this can be easier said than done. Marketing, especially professional marketing services, can take a considerable investment of time and money, but it doesn't have to be expensive to be effective. Figure 7.2 reflects a list of free or low-cost marketing strategies compiled by the staff at Cornell University's CTL.

Figure 7.2. Free or low-cost marketing strategies for educational developers.

→ **Make contact with faculty**
- Send a "welcome" note to all new faculty members
- Send out an online survey to determine faculty needs and interests
- Hold an online chat with faculty
- Adapt your programming to meet faculty needs and let them know you are responsive
- Hold a focus group or faculty planning committee meeting for events
- Hold a brown bag lunch on a topic of interest for faculty
- Hold an open house
- Celebrate faculty teaching accomplishments by spotlighting them on your website or by establishing excellence in teaching awards
- Identify and build a relationship with a "champion" in each department
- Provide a tip or a useful tool to department champions to share with colleagues
- Call faculty who might be interested before each event

→ **Use your website and social media**
- Update your website homepage frequently
- Create a blog for your website with a tip for the day or other useful information
- Feature faculty teaching innovations and accomplishments on your website
- Create an online survey to show faculty that you are interested in their input
- Post testimonials from faculty members on your website
- Use tools such as LinkedIn, Facebook, Twitter, and Google+ to create a social network and encourage faculty to follow you
- Update and tweet to promote events, to link interesting information, and to stimulate discussion

→ **Try and find volunteer help (marketing takes time and effort)**
- Partner with a marketing class, allowing students to complete marketing initiatives as part of their coursework
- Award volunteers with a certificate attesting to skills developed

→ **Remember**
- Always seek out networking opportunities (get one or more names from every contact)
- The best marketing is positive word-of-mouth for providing excellent programs, resources, and support

Source: Pettit and Kenyon, 2012.

Communication Function 2: Getting Them in the Door (Persuasion)

The primary purpose of your marketing and branding efforts is to get the word out and let people know who you are and what you do, but a communication plan has other functions, and one of the primary ones is to get people in the door and participating in your events and programs. Previous Taking Flight participants rank this among their highest priorities—not building the center, but getting people to come. This requires you to persuade them that the work you do matters to them, to their students, and to the institution. In this sense, your communication plan serves an explicitly rhetorical function, one in which you want to consider how you can change what we often call the educational development value proposition.

The value proposition is based on rational choice theory, which states that people make decisions based on the *information* they have available about what *actions* will enable them to fulfill their *interests*. That information forms the basis of a cost-benefit analysis that we all, at least in theory, use to choose what actions we will actually take (Allingham, 2001; Fernández-Huerga, 2008). If you want to change the actions people take, the theory suggests that you need to change one of these three components, either by increasing the perceived benefits, utility, or interest in what you'd like them to do. If you'd like more faculty to avail themselves of your services, for example, then you need to use your communication strategy to increase perceived benefits, utility, or interest in order to increase the value they place on your programs. If this sounds complicated, it isn't. What you basically have to do is identify good reasons why faculty should choose to engage in faculty development (or teaching transformation), and those reasons have to be sufficiently persuasive that they choose to rank these preferences higher than other ways in which they could be spending their time. In other words, you aren't just trying to persuade them to attend your events; you're trying to persuade them what to give up, or devalue, in order to spend time on teaching and learning. Finding just the right reasons, though, is a considerable challenge.

Scholars in rhetorical studies have suggested that there are four primary persuasion challenges that need to be overcome in order to get someone to change their value equation (Eisend, 2007; O'Keefe, 2016). In the following sections, we will talk about those challenges in the context of faculty development and suggest some strategies for addressing each one.

Persuasion Challenge 1: Faculty (or Other Stakeholders) May Not See the Positive Value of Your Work

Strategy 1: You can change the information they have available.

There is a common misconception that faculty development does not have a strong evidence base, but that is simply not the case. Mary Wright and her coauthors created an issue of *POD Speaks* in which they provided, in a short and readable format, a summary of the considerable body of research evidence that shows that time spent on faculty development can make a substantive impact on teaching practice (Finelli et al., 2008) and student learning (Condon et al., 2016; Gibbs & Coffey, 2004) in the short and long term and across different contexts (Wright et al., 2018). And there are studies that meet standards for rigorous social science methods, including large populations, control groups, and quasi experimental designs (Connolly, Savoy, Lee, & Hill, 2016; Freeman et al., 2014). This is communication intended to flip the value proposition on its head.

Strategy 2: You can address potential counterarguments or reasons to devalue faculty development work. This involves overturning some common negative assumptions.

Common assumption 1: We are a repair shop where you send your broken faculty.

Counterargument: Educational development has worked hard to come up with very intentional ways to separate itself from serving a primarily remedial role, and CTL directors are adept at navigating the balance between working (discretely) with those faculty who are in a position to receive formal intervention and with all faculty, regardless of level of teaching expertise. A CTL is fundamentally a unit of faculty development, which means that it works to meet faculty where they are and to elevate them to new places. Even the best teachers want to, and can, continue to enhance their teaching knowledge and practice. Effective student learning rests on elevating teaching, not just teachers. It might help if you could get your best teachers on board and encourage them to tell their peers about what you're doing.

Common assumption 2: We are primarily here to provide tips, tricks, and easy fixes.

Counterargument: The evidence base for teaching and learning practice is rich and robust, but it does not provide clear and easy answers, and rarely does it suggest panaceas. You can lure people in the door with the promise of quick solutions, but you'll change hearts and minds by engaging them deeply, even intellectually, in the complexities, ambiguities, and challenges of teaching in their discipline.

Common assumption 3: We will judge you for not teaching the "right way."

Counterargument: The research on faculty motivation strongly points away from the provision of overly prescriptive, unqualified, or top-down models for encouraging faculty to change their teaching practice. This is sometimes referred to as "preaching about teaching." Instead, what we do is provide the equivalent of food for thought and give faculty the autonomy and flexibility to adapt what we learn from the literature into the context of their disciplines, their classrooms, and their own approach to teaching. Our goal is not to have everyone teach the same way; rather, our goal is to turn everyone into reflective practitioners who want to, who choose to, continually adapt their teaching to maximize the student learning experience (Schön, 2017).

Persuasion Challenge 2: What Other People Say

In this case, faculty may see the value changing their teaching, but because they don't see other people doing it (descriptive norms) or they believe that others don't want them to do it (prescriptive norms), they do not work with you to make those changes. They're concerned about standing out, and not in a good way (Bond et al., 2012; Cialdini et al., 2006).

Strategy 1: You can simply change the information they have available. In the case of descriptive norms, simply let ambivalent or concerned faculty know that other faculty do participate in faculty development, and not just faculty who need help (see previous assumption). Make sure you disseminate your participation numbers. Take photos at your events and publish them in the campus newspaper. Place video testimonials on your website. Highlight SoTL projects being done on your campus. Ask teaching award winners to mention your support in their acceptance speeches.

Strategy 2: You can help them change their beliefs about what matters (and to whom). If they think faculty development is not valued in their department, then you can show them that it is indeed valued by the college, the institution, the field, and/or the students. Point to your alignment with the university's strategic plan (see chapter 5), have them talk to a supportive colleague in their college, ply them with research literature, and highlight specific feedback students have given. Some CTLs are now including students as part of their course redesign teams, which can serve as an additional incentive. Throw the department a bone by giving the faculty member a familiar-sounding role (e.g., fellow, board member) to document their involvement.

Strategy 3: You can change what other people think. This is harder, of course, but it can help you to think beyond the level of individual support. You can provide models for how faculty document their work in teaching and learning as part of their tenure and reappointment portfolios. You can provide educational resources for tenure or evaluation committees. You can partner with other campus units to change policies and procedures that recognize and reward teaching transformation, including teaching awards, portfolios, and evaluations.

Persuasion Challenge 3: They Can't Do It

Sometimes people don't want to be persuaded to change because they don't believe they have the skills or ability to do it well. We've mentioned imposter syndrome before, but academia is rife with it, especially in teaching where many faculty have received little to no formal training (Hagen, Gutkin, Wilson, & Oats, 1998).

Strategy 1: It can help to remove obstacles that may be standing in the way, such as fear of negative repercussions for trying something new and it not working perfectly. Some course design programs provide faculty with an evaluation "pass" for the first time they teach a redesigned course. Other CTLs provide documentation (suitable for inclusion in evaluation files) that teaching transformation often starts with a dip in evaluations followed by a significant upturn.

Strategy 2: You might want to consider providing models to show reluctant faculty members that, yes, it can be done by people like you and for students like yours. This often means selecting disciplinary peers (possibly broad disciplinary buckets, such as STEM or social sciences), and likely disciplinary peers at your institution, or one similar to it. You could institute an open classroom project, for example, where faculty can sign up to be observed (informally) by their peers or to do the observing.

Strategy 3: You could have them try a few baby steps, an activity to rehearse what they might do for real in their own classroom. Some CTLs, for example, have classroom laboratory spaces for faculty to try out new methods. Graduate student teaching programs often include microteaching, where new instructors teach a subject for a set period of time (either in person or by videotape) and then receive critique from peers and a CTL facilitator. On a smaller scale, role-playing can be effective, especially if you are able to keep the proposed activity contained to a manageable level, perhaps even a change that takes up only, say, 10 minutes of class time, similar to James Lang's concept of small teaching (Lang, 2016). If they can do one small change the hope is that the small change will lead to the next one, and the next.

Persuasion Challenge 4: Good Idea, But . . .

For this final persuasion challenge, you may have faculty who think working on their teaching is a great idea, and they feel capable and supported in doing so, but somehow those good intentions never quite get translated into actual action. We've all done this, of course, in some aspect of our lives, so you might want to ask yourself what strategies worked for you when you finally quit smoking, lost weight, ate healthier, spent more time with your kids, and so on. This may sound trite, but studies have shown that strategies to influence wellness factors, such as those just mentioned, can be effectively applied to other contexts, including faculty development (Head & Noar, 2014).

Strategy 1: Give faculty a nudge.

You can provide prompts, just simple reminders or cues, to induce behavior (Fry & Neff, 2009). These can take the form of emails (e.g., We're approaching midsemester, time to schedule your small-group analysis session), signs (e.g., elements of a learning-centered syllabus; Cox, Cox, & Cox, 2000), or timely suggestions (e.g., a newsletter item that features ideas for conducting effective study sessions near the end of a semester).

Strategy 2: Baby Steps

Encourage faculty to articulate the concrete step(s) they plan to take to turn their good intentions into action. This may sound a bit silly at first, but the research is clear that saying or writing down what you intend to do significantly increases the chances that you will actually do it (Gollwitzer & Sheeran, 2006; Hagger & Luszczynska, 2014). This can be as simple as asking participants to write down (perhaps on an index card) what steps they will take to implement what they've learned, or it can be as complex as developing a department-focused five-year plan for teaching transformation.

Communication Function 3: Hitting Your Targets (Strategic Communication)

Much of our work as educational developers is about relationships, and the key to any healthy relationship is communication. In "Achieving a Culture of Communication on Campus," Richard K. Boyer (2016) reflects on the consequences of effective and ineffective communication in the midst of campus crises and social unrest to develop the argument that successful universities exhibit a "culture of communication." He posits that "a culture of communication is about using the right techniques to engage the right audience about a relevant topic at the optimal time." He regards this as a "strategic alliance of communication channel, audience topic, and timing" (Boyer, 2016. Para 5).

Once you've established your marketing strategy and persuaded people of your value, the next step is to consider strategic ways to target your message toward specific audiences. A common phenomenon across institutional context is that different stakeholders usually only want to read/hear/see what they are interested in, which requires a series of well-thought-out targeted solutions. As noted previously, we are not an island, and so we use communication to show how we are meeting the needs of the campus, strengthen our networks, advocate for our work, and to do all of these in our distinctive organizational context.

In a rather simple representation of the university structure we can identify a number of groups we need to target in Figure 7.3.

Ordinarily, we tend to focus a lot of our attention—too much, perhaps—on leadership. Understandably, we look to those who most directly support and evaluate us, not simply to impress them but to align with them and to explore, together, ways to enhance our alignment with other units, programs,

Figure 7.3. Communication plan target diagram.

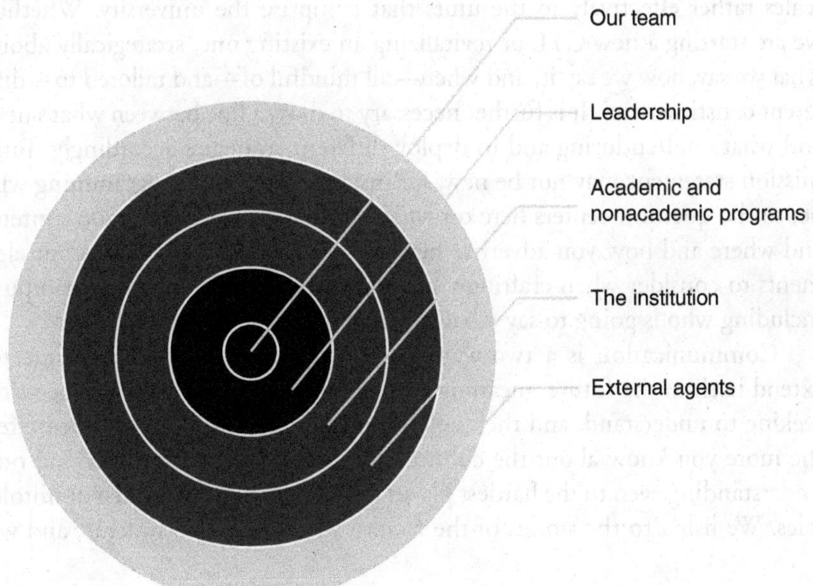

Our team

Leadership

Academic and nonacademic programs

The institution

External agents

Ask Yourself:

Based on what you've just learned about rhetorical strategies for communication in educational development:

- What is one step you are going to take to implement what you've learned *by next week?*
- What is one step you are going to take to implement what you've learned *over the next month?*
- What is one step you are going to take to implement what you've learned *over the next year?*

and initiatives on campus. We also focus a lot on our strategic partners, sometimes with a limited view of who they are and can be. If we wish to develop a systematic communication plan, we should think in terms of expanding our breadth and depth.

Once you have identified your constituents and the types of communication to use; you can now target your message (What do our constituents want to know?) and align your strategy (What do we want our constituents to know?). The example in Worksheet 7.1 comes from Penn State's Schreyer Institute for Teaching Excellence, but you can adapt it for use on any campus.

Although Boyer's primary unit of analysis is the university, his approach scales rather effectively to the units that comprise the university. Whether we are starting a new CTL or revitalizing an existing one, strategically about what we say, how we say it, and when—all mindful of—and tailored to—different constituencies. It is further necessary to draw a line between what's new and what's old/enduring and to deploy different strategies accordingly. Your mission statement may not be new, for instance, but your programming will be, so the question centers here on where and how you curate static content and where and how you advertise new content. Worksheet 7.2 lays out elements to consider when crafting your ongoing communications to campus, including who is going to say what to whom.

Communication is a two-way street, and that street will continue to extend itself in the future, meaning that our work is continually a process of seeking to understand, and then being understood. Your work will be better the more you know about the culture of your institution, so we extend our understanding even to the hardest places to reach, including hidden or untold tales. We listen to the stories of the faculty who teach our students, and we

WORKSHEET 7.1
Constituents Communication Matrix

Constituents	What do our constituents want to know?	What do we want our constituents to know?
EXAMPLE: Department Chairs and Program Heads	• What we do and how that will help faculty • How effectively we work with faculty facing teaching challenges • Whether we take referrals	• People in their college and department already work with us • Principles that guide our practice • Process of working with us

Note: Table designed by Angela Linse, used with her permission.

WORKSHEET 7.2
Strategic Communication Matrix

For each topic define as many as you can—Identify and address the:	
Sample Topic: A new faculty learning community on civility	
Message: What is the message? Why does this topic matter? Why now? What is a faculty learning community? Potential audiences?	
Messenger(s) Who should create and deliver the message?	
Relayers Who else can convey the message? Where? Why? How?	
Audience(s) Who are secondary, and tertiary populations? Who might you be missing?	
Channels What are the dominant (institutional) and actual channels/pathways to your audiences?	
Techniques What is the best way to communicate with each audience? Focus on general and custom techniques. Walk-by conversations? Email? Calendar invitations?	
Timing When is the best time to schedule an event? When are the best times to advertise an event to maximize attention? Find the fulcrum between not enough and too much information. Think: when it's new, when it's coming up, and sometime in-between to sustain interest.	
Closing the loop: A plan to address feedback We will get feedback from faculty. How do you handle the positive, the negative, the indifferent, and the pushback? What about non-communication?	

TABLE 7.2

Constituents for a CTL Communication Plan

Constituents	Communication Methods
Internal In this field we identify, share, and leverage the unique skills and accomplishments of our team.	Formal presentations Data gathering and analysis on programming, LMS usage, etc. Data visualization (e.g., high-impact graphics) CTL intranet Posters/motivational or celebratory artifacts T-Shirts, pins, or other wearable artifacts
Leadership In this field we identify our academic leaders, what they need to know, from whom, when, and how. Example: Chief academic officer/provost	Annual reports. Brief reports/quarterly updates Highlights (often in the form of sound bites or bullet points) Media artifacts (videos, news reports, radio spots)
Programs In this field we identify existing and potential collaborative units and programs on campus, mindful of our academic partners. Academic Nonacademic Example Office of Service-Learning, community leadership programs	Unit-focused presentations Audience-based social media Resource guides
Campus In this field we identify how, when, and where we need to enhance our general visibility through our actions. Example Faculty Senate	Newsletters Flyers/brochures Posters CTL website Campus conversations. Conferences
External/Beyond In this field we identify persons, programs, and institutions, with whom we can collaborate or through whom we can enhance our impact. Example Board of Trustees	Advancement and capital campaigns to gather resources, foundation accounts, named programs, and so on. Conferences Professional organizations Publishing opportunities Grants and research Regional consortia Multi-institutional collaborations

share in their triumphs and find solace in their defeats. And then, after we listen, we relate, respond, and become productively enmeshed in the grand narrative (Bowen, 2012).

You can become the protagonist, even at times the hero, of your story. You can use what you've heard to connect our message and our work to others, groups or individuals, and to become indispensable to their success. Educational development is fundamentally an other-directed enterprise—we exist to support and advance the mission and the people who define and comprise the institution. We do this by effectively promoting programs and services, by getting faculty to be a part of those programs, and by giving the right people the right information to shape the campus culture. By finding a variety of means, strategies, and audiences for telling our story, we put ourselves in the position to be part of happily ever after.

8

ASSESSMENT

How Will You Know When You Get There?

There is a Calvin and Hobbes cartoon in which Calvin is trying, with some degree of frustration, to learn how to manipulate a yo-yo. In the final panel, he turns to the reader and states, "I can't imagine mastering the skills involved here without a clearer understanding of who's going to be impressed." This cartoon crops up frequently in Internet searches when the terms *assessment* and *humor* are tagged, a search we did when considering how to introduce this subject in *Taking Flight*. We thought these examples might be helpful in setting the tone because for many people assessment is no laughing matter.

This unfortunate perception likely comes from several sources. A major contributor is that the majority of us have little to no professional training in program assessment, which can feel as if you are starting at a deficit before you begin. Assessment can be difficult and time-consuming work that requires expertise to conduct effectively. The practice and research literature of assessment is voluminous and grows exponentially all the time—the references for this chapter only scratch the surface (Ambrosino & Peel, 2011; Chalmers & Gardiner, 2015; Hines, 2009b; Nadler, Shore, Taylor, & Bakker, 2012; Peresellin & Goodrick, 2010; Ruben, 2005). Most of us are accustomed to serving as experts in our respective areas, and it can be humbling and uncomfortable to find ourselves back at the level of novice.

You may say you *do* have experience in assessment, perhaps in assessing learning in your courses or even as part of your department or program evaluation process. While both are useful, the assessment of educational development has distinct challenges and functions beyond the measurement of learning outcomes. It is perhaps no wonder that workshops and interactive sessions on assessing our work continue to be the most highly attended—and valued—at professional conferences and are an integral aspect of training for new members of the field (Collins-Brown et al., 2016; Hines, 2009a).

Assessment often feels like it is being imposed from outside and like we have limited control over whether or how to do it. This state of affairs is reflected in its discourse, which makes uses of terms such as *burden* or *compliance*. This discourse is grounded in the fact that the stakes for assessment can be high. In what has been deemed by some scholars as the age of accountability for higher education, the proliferation of publically accessible assessment is a necessary by-product (Beach et al., 2016; Shulman, 2007). Failure to meet required assessment standards or criteria can have dire consequences, including loss of prestige, funding, position, rank, or even accreditation. This approach differs in fundamental ways from the formative, developmental, and confidential approach that characterizes much of the field of educational development.

Hopefully, we haven't gotten you so discouraged about assessment that you have stopped reading, because the good news is that assessment, rather than being a burden, can also be your ally, and you can conduct it in a manner that is compatible with our professional values. As of 2018, there is a growing call for standardized assessments of educational development that cross over multiple institutional contexts in higher education (American Council on Education, 2017), but currently there are no widely accepted external standards or criteria. While this may mean you do not have a clear set of guidelines that you can simply copy and paste to your context, it also means that you do have agency over how and to what extent you assess your work, and you can be a part of ongoing conversations about what assessment can do to influence a culture of teaching and learning, both for your center and institution. To put it another way, not only will there be people who are impressed by your ability to master this yo-yo, but you may find yourself teaching others new tricks.

The Assessment Dilemma in Educational Development

In their seminal overview of the field of educational development, Mary Dean Sorcinelli and her coauthors delineate a number of historical ages, starting with the teacher in the 1960s and ending with our current age of accountability and assessment (Beach et al., 2016; Sorcinelli et al., 2006). Numerous factors fuel the need for more assessment, including the current financial crisis in higher education, which is felt perhaps most keenly by public institutions, who are seeing marked declines in state-sponsored support, and small liberal arts colleges, a number of which are struggling for survival. What this means is that universities have to take every step they can to ensure that increasingly precious funds are being used as efficiently and effectively as possible. Support for faculty development is not an exception. The impetus also comes from within our field, as assessment shapes and legitimizes the expansion of our role(s) within higher education. It seems inescapable that in this day and age you will need to plan to spend a significant amount of time designing, implementing, applying, and communicating the results of your assessment plan.

As mentioned previously, this may be easier said than done. There is a central assessment dilemma that lies at the heart of educational development (Sutherland & Hill, 2018). One of the guiding principles of assessment is alignment, and the mark of high-quality assessment is how closely (and accurately) you can measure what you are actually trying to assess. Herein lies our dilemma. In educational development, we primarily work with faculty (whether individually or in groups or units) who then apply what they have learned to improve student learning. If we consider improved student learning as one of our primary end goals, our impact is, at best, indirect, and our influence is mitigated through many potentially confounding factors that are beyond our control. In addition to these challenges to our assessment design, we also have fundamental issues with construct validity, as the definition of *good* teaching and learning in higher education is complex, hotly contested, and often highly politicized. Despite all of these challenges, what our situation boils down to is the need to be thoughtful, creative, and flexible as we master the art of assessment.

Assessment: A Multilayered Cake

Because of our dilemma, the assessment of educational development often resembles a layer cake, with multiple levels and types of evidence, many of which are stacked on top of each other to produce a result that hopefully you will want to both have and eat. In this section, we break down some of the more significant layers of the cake and suggest possible recipes, or solutions, that vary by level of expertise and/or sophistication (including starting point, next level, and advanced). If you are just starting, for example, you may wish to follow the suggestions at the level of starting point; then simply add appropriate measures drawn from the higher levels as you and your center grow (see Figure 8.1).

Layer 1: Document

In this age of accountability, you will likely have multiple occasions for which you will need to document the nature and extent of the work that you do.

Figure 8.1. Educational development assessment layer cake.

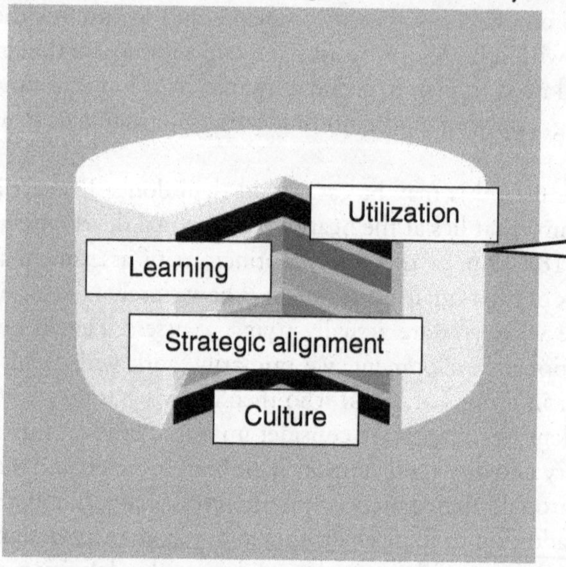

Source. Photo copyright Shutterstock.com, used by license.

This layer of assessment can be useful in ensuring that you are in compliance with the university norms, justifying resources or resource requests based on workload, or simply responding to inquiries from others who may not be aware of the full extent of what CTLs do.

To fulfill this purpose, most CTLs make use of *utilization-focused assessment*, a somewhat fancy term for simply keeping track of useful information (Patton, 2008), such as the number of services provided and the people they serve, often done in the form of simple counts. For example, you might document, "We provided consultation services to 87 faculty in the spring semester of 2016." You may also wish to show that those services were valuable to the faculty who availed themselves of it, a measurement that is frequently captured through the use of satisfaction surveys, provided after an event or service has been provided and/or as part of an annual survey. Figure 8.2 provides a sample template, although, like many CTL surveys, it asks for more than just satisfaction information (so the name is a bit misleading). These methods have the advantages of being simple to implement, easy to manage, and relatively transparent in meaning (Belanger, Belisle, & Bernatches, 2011). For these reasons, using these two measurements together can be an appropriate place to start building your portfolio of assessment measures.

You may find, however, that simply keeping track of numbers limits your ability to demonstrate your engagement with targeted audiences.

Figure 8.2. Event evaluation form (satisfaction).

---

1. Please rate the content of this program.

1	2	3	4	5
Not Valuable	Somewhat Valuable	Neutral Valuable	Valuable	Extremely

Comments?

2. Please rate the usefulness of this program.

1	2	3	4	5
Not Useful	Somewhat Useful	Neutral	Useful	Extremely Useful

Comments?

3. Do you plan to implement at least one thing that you learned in today's workshop?

          Yes   No   Not Applicable

If yes, what will that be?

4. What is the most valuable thing you will take away from the program?

5. What would you recommend we change regarding this program?

Note: Designed by Bruce Kelley and Taimi Olsen for the POD Network's 2015 Institute for New Faculty Developers. Used with their permission.

While the provost, for example, may be interested in the total number of faculty you serve, the dean of the College of Business wants to know how many of his her faculty you serve. To take your assessment efforts to the next level, you may wish to capture a wider range of information about your clientele that would enable you to respond requests like that of the dean's, as well as descriptive statistics to characterize patterns and trends within your usage data. A list of potential variables (all of which have been collected by at least one other CTL) is included in Figure 8.3. While you can glean most of these data from institutional sources, the process of collecting data can quickly become burdensome as your number of clients grows. Many CTLs choose instead to collect these data from faculty directly, often as part of a standardized registration process for services or events.

Figure 8.3. Demographic variables for CTL assessment.

Name (unique user)
Department, college
Discipline
Rank
Years at the institution
Primary instructional site/location
Primary instructional mode of delivery (e.g. online, face-to-face,
    hybrid)
Average class size
Teaching and learning publications
Teaching awards
Service/event attended
Role in event (e.g. speaker/presenter, participant)
Gender preference
Race/ethnicity

When you are just starting out, it can be relatively easy to keep track of your services, but as time goes by, you may find yourself contending with a larger number of people and services in any given year or semester, compounded by the existence of multiple years of data. It does not take long before you have a data management problem (Godert & Kenyon, 2013). To alleviate this problem, many centers have had success with incorporating software programs that are specifically designed to keep track of and process this kind of information. Your institution may even already subscribe to such a tracking and ticketing system, as they are frequently used by offices such as an IT help desk, tutoring/student services centers, or libraries. You should be prepared to spend time on developing the appropriate parameters, categories, and processes that will make your system function in a manner that will not only provide you with useful assessment data immediately but also grow with you and your successors and be sustained over the long term.

Layer 2: Learning Outcomes

Utilization-based assessment does have its limitations (Milloy & Brooke, 2004). You may be able to demonstrate, for example, that someone attended one of your events, but a head count does not differentiate between a faculty member who slept through the whole thing and someone who transforms every aspect of their teaching based on what they learned. Fortunately, we have a familiar model for looking at impact that is based on what we teach faculty about gauging their effectiveness in the classroom: outcomes-based assessment (Brooks, March, Wilcox, & Cohen, 2011). To engage in this kind of assessment, it is necessary to articulate learning outcomes for your events, programs, or initiatives and then determine appropriate measures to gauge the degree to which you have achieved them. This kind of assessment can range from applying an outcomes-centered design to an event evaluation form (see Table 8.1) to a more comprehensive collection of artifacts and evidence (Hines, 2011; Hurney, Brantmeier, Good, Harrison, & Meizner, 2016; Klodiana & Anstey, 2017; Plank & Kalish, 2010).

Like classroom assessment, outcomes-based assessment for CTLs can serve as a powerful tool for improving the work that you do (Kelley, 2018). It can also function as formative assessment for you and your team, especially as you prepare for the next iteration of events, or as an evidence base from which to make decisions regarding priorities for time and resources. Utilization numbers (as discussed in Layer 1): Document can also serve a formative function, especially if you review them for trends or patterns that

TABLE 8.1
Outcomes-Based Session Evaluation Template

After completing this session, you will be able to:
- Understand the definition and uses of. . . .
- Strategize ways to engage in. . . .
- Articulate goals for planning. . . .

Session:	Strongly Disagree				Strongly Agree
Based on this session, I understand the definition and uses of. . . .	1	2	3	4	5
Based on this session, I have learned strategic ways to engage in. . . .	1	2	3	4	5
Based on this session, I have a plan for integrating my goals for. . . .	1	2	3	4	5
This session provided me with new knowledge or skills.	1	2	3	4	5
I will be able to apply what I have learned in this session to my teaching.	1	2	3	4	5

Note: Designed by Bruce Kelley and Taimi Olsen for the POD Network's 2015 Institute for New Faculty Developers. Used with their permission.

may be emerging, or for identifying potential gaps in your services that you might wish to address. That being said, participation rates alone do not provide sufficient insight into how faculty are actually using what they have learned from you.

As in classroom assessment, where one of the most powerful forms of evidence for learning outcomes can be in the form of student artifacts, another source of data for the teaching outcomes of your CTL is the collection of faculty artifacts, such as revised syllabi, new instructional materials, multimedia presentations, published scholarship, or statements of teaching philosophy. This kind of assessment can be considerably more time-consuming to systematically analyze than utilization data, but it can also provide richer fodder for adapting your programs and services to most effectively influence changes in teaching practice.

Artifacts that reflect student learning outcomes can also be valuable to you, but they have limitations (Gibbs & Coffey, 2004). You, or perhaps your supervisor, may be tempted to utilize student evaluations of instruction (SETs) as a form of evidence for your outcomes-based assessment plan. After all, these appear to provide an external measure of the success of improved teaching methods. Analysis of SET data is most often done comparatively, either by looking at improvements made by individual faculty before and after working with you, or through a more global perspective, looking at the differentials between faculty who have utilized your services versus those who have not. Even when we put aside the controversies surrounding student evaluations of instructions as a measure of teaching effectiveness, the use of this data is fraught with challenges and dangers.

The challenge lies in adapting an instrument that is not intended to be used for this purpose. For example, SETs are intended to provide feedback on a number of markers of teaching effectiveness, but the faculty member may have come to you for advice and support on a more limited issue. Several CTLs have had success with a partial solution, in which they limit their assessment to only those questions in the SET that are most applicable, or sensitive, to faculty development. Textbook selection, for example, is likely to be largely out of your purview, but use of active learning or educational technology may be right in your wheelhouse. Others have taken the opportunity to advocate for the inclusion of an additional question or questions on the SET that could provide insight into their effectiveness.

That being said, the challenge of using SETs as evidence stems from the myriad of variables and influences that affect student perceptions of teaching and learning, and how few of those are likely to be directly attributable to the work of your CTL. There are no easy ways to mitigate this challenge, and, for this reason, a number of educational developers advocate that SETs not be used to assess their work, or be used only with great caution and care.

Layer 3: Strategic Alignment

Outcomes-based assessment, in the second layer of our assessment cake, provides us with useful insight into the effectiveness of our events and programs. Like utilization data, it is not without limitations. First, it tends to be retrospective, telling us more about how we have been doing in the past rather than what we could be doing in the future. Second, it is primarily a measure of our individual programs and services, which are part of the work of what a center does, but may not capture all of what do, or aspire to do. This is especially the case as the field continues to move away from the view of a CTL as primarily a provider of a slate of services and instead serves a more holistic role of advancing the teaching and learning mission of the university (Hurney et al., 2016). In the third layer, we consider comprehensive assessment that looks to measure your contributions to the strategic goals of your center and the institution, with an emphasis on increasing the perceived value of your work.

At the starting point, this layer of assessment should be closely tied to your own strategic planning efforts (see chapter 5 of this volume for more information on the strategic planning process). For each facet of your mission and strategic goals, it is suggested that you gather data/evidence to demonstrate the degree to which you have achieved these goals over a given period (often an academic year). See Table 8.2 for a template to help you think through this process.

For the purposes of strategic assessment, you can consider still using your participation and outcomes-based program data, but it can help to reframe it in a strategic context. For example, if one of your strategic goals is to promote teaching transformation across your campus, simply listing the number of faculty, although useful in some contexts, does not provide sufficient evidence of changes to the depth of your impact (Kreber & Brook, 2001).

Measures of strategic impact, such as these just listed, lend themselves well to data visualization, such as pie charts or graphs, suitable for inclusion in formal documents used for summative assessment purposes, such as performance evaluations, CTL annual reports, and presentations to stakeholder groups.

Speaking of stakeholder groups, the next level of comprehensive assessment focuses on increasing your understanding of stakeholder needs and extending that understanding to an informed vision of the overall faculty development needs of your institution. To achieve these deeper levels of

TABLE 8.2
Principles for Strategic Assessment

Principle:	Answer for your CTL:
#1a: Identify the strategic goals of your institution that directly bear on the activities of your center. (*from chapter 4*)	
#1b: With 1a in mind, identify the key organizational goals for your center. (*from chapter 4*)	
#2: Identify two or three outcomes for each organizational goal.	
#3: Identify ways to collect data relevant to the outcomes identified in #2.	
#4: Identify the limitations of your data.	
#5: Based on your responses from #4, how might you improve?	
#6: Tell your story! Identify who the key individuals are at your institution that need to hear about your success. (*from chapter 6*)	

Note: Designed by Bruce Kelley and Taimi Olsen for the POD Network's 2015 Institute for New Faculty Developers. Used with their permission.

Ask Yourself:

- What if you look at the number of faculty you serve relative to the total number of faculty, and demonstrate that the ratio is growing over time?
- What if you look at changes in the breadth of your services? In other words, who you are reaching that perhaps you had not reached before? How many disciplines, departments, colleges, ranks, or other demographic variables are represented?
- What if instead of only rating satisfaction with your services, you also asked a simple yes/no (or open-ended) question on your annual survey and/or follow-up surveys for events and services in which faculty state whether or not they changed something in their teaching practice based on their interaction with your CTL?

empathy, many CTLs engage in qualitative assessment, including interviews, focus groups, listening tours, and ethnographic observation. A listening tour, for example, involves arranging to meet with stakeholder or constituent groups, perhaps as part of their standard meeting schedule; asking a series of targeted questions; and listening to (and recording) the results. Ethnographic observation may consist of shadowing faculty members as they develop and teach their courses.

A word of caution: Conducting this kind of assessment takes a considerable investment of time and effort, often well beyond the demands of data collection or analysis of artifacts (the first two layers). It is a common mistake to underestimate how much time these kinds of activities take, as we tend to forget how much preplanning is needed to identify participants, schedule the sessions, and get institutional review board approval (if needed) and how much postinterview work is needed to obtain useable data, including transcription, coding, and analysis. In the end, it may be worth it, as your efforts will lead to the development of a bigger—and better—picture of the needs of your network and how you can strategically enhance your visibility within it (see Figure 8.4). All of this hard work can have benefits beyond assessment, too, as various listening sessions can serve double-duty as opportunities for promoting greater understanding of your work as well as strengthening your constituent relationships.

As you advance and your center matures, your strategic planning and assessment should become increasingly closely tied to the mission and strategic plan of your institution, which means that it becomes increasingly difficult for us to provide you with general practices that apply across the wide variety of institutional contexts that characterize the landscape of contemporary higher education (Kelley et al., 2017; Kezar & Eckel, 2002). What works for a community college, for example, may not work at a small liberal arts campus or a large research-intensive university. That being said, several scholars have articulated a number of widely applicable principles of good assessment practice that you may consult as you continue to revise, adapt, and refine your assessment plan at regular intervals. One example of a set of program assessment principles (from prominent higher education researcher Sue Hines) is presented in Figure 8.4, but it should be emphasized that our field does not have a single set of principles or frameworks that has been accepted CTL-wide, so there are other examples in the literature that you may find equally useful (see bibliography online for more of these).[1]

One of the central principles in Hines's schema is the emphasis on multiple sources of evidence, a mantra that is often repeated in research and practice on assessment in educational development, including in the lessons from this chapter (Plank, Kalish, Rohdieck, & Harper, 2005). It can be challenging to juggle these sources and keep track of their alignment to your strategic goals, so you may wish to make use of an assessment matrix, similar to the example in Table 8.3, which serves to bring your assessment work all together and allows you to get a snapshot of the range and value of what you are collecting. Because every institution is different, the rows and columns of your

Figure 8.4. 8 dimensions of quality program assessment.

1. Systematic: Creates feedback from systemic and continuous assessment.
2. Goal-directed: Clear program goals guide the assessment.
3. Measurable objectives: Objectives are designed in ways that enable measurement.
4. Criteria for success: Standards have been set that define the desired level of goal achievement.
5. Assessment methods measure the objectives: The methods are valid measures of the objectives.
6. Multiple measures: The assessment uses multiple measures of program quality.
7. Summative and formative data: The data gathered can serve the purposes of both program improvement and a determination of end-of-program effectiveness.
8. Evidence of a causal relationship: Uses comparative data to establish a causal relationship between program activities and its impact(s).

Source: Hines, S. R. 2009. "Investigating Faculty Development Program Assessment Practices: What's Being Done and How Can It Be Improved?" *Journal of Faculty Development 23* (3): 5-19.

TABLE 8.3

How CRLT Evaluates Its Own Programs and Services

	Event sign-ins & service reports from CRLT staff	Website hits	Immediate feedback questionnaires	Follow-up email & online surveys	Participant reports & narratives	Interviews & focus groups	Measurement of Teaching Outcomes
How many clients (administrative, faculty and graduate students) does CRLT serve?	X (Analyzed by demographics)	X (Analyzed by on- and off-campus hits)					
How valuable/useful do participants find CRLT services?			X (e.g., At all workshops, participants rate the overall value of the session)	X (e.g., New Faculty Orientation and Provost's Seminar on Teaching attendees receive an email, asking them to rate the overall value of the event)	X (Emails and conversations)	X (e.g., Campus Leadership Program participants)	
What changes do instructors report they will make or have made in their teaching as a result of a CRLT service/program?			X (e.g., Theater sketch attendees are asked what they learned that will apply to their work with students)	X (e.g., Midterm Student Feedback clients are asked about changes they made in their course as a result of the service; pre- and posttest student of Teaching Academy participants' sense of preparation for teaching)	X (e.g., Project reports from recipients of larger CRLT grants)	X (e.g., Interviews and focus groups with faculty/administrators about instructional and organizational changes stemming from theater performances)	X (e.g., Pre- and posttest study of the impact of different feedback services on student ratings; Investigating Student Learning poster analysis)

TABLE 8.3 (*Continued*)

	X	X	X
What has been the long-term impact of CRLT services/programs on participants' attitudes/behaviors?	(e.g., Survey of Graduate Teaching Consultants about impact of the program on their instructional and mentoring work as faculty)	(e.g., Teaching with Technology Institute and Teagle presentations)	(e.g., Interviews in China with Michigan-China University Leadership Forum participants)
	X	X	X
What needs are there at the University of Michigan for new programs and services?	(e.g., Surveys of graduate students to assess the need for a Preparing Future Faculty Seminar and information technology training)	(e.g., Attendees at TA mentoring events asked to suggest new initiatives)	(e.g., Initial needs assessment for Campus Leadership Forum)

Source: Mary Wright, Mary Wright@brown.edu (Created at CRLT, University of Michigan); Distributed at POD Network NED 2017 goo.nl/xY6cYL; Wright, M.C. (2011). Measuring a teaching center's effectiveness. In C.E. Cook & M. Kaplan, Eds. *Advancing the culture of teaching on campus: How a teaching center can make a difference* (pp. 28-49). Sterling, VA: Stylus. Reprinted with permission.

matrix will most likely vary from those of a large and well-established center, but you are encouraged to adapt this tool as a means for integrating your own distinctive blend of assessment questions and evidence.

Layer 4: Role Model

To recap the layers of our assessment cake so far, the collection and dissemination of your assessment data serves to document the extent and impact of your work, inform your own internal decision-making, align your work with your mission, and demonstrate your strategic value to the campus. You could also say that it might serve one final purpose that could be described as an ulterior motive: to serve as a role model for the values and norms that we would like to see become part of the organizational culture of our own institutions and perhaps even across higher education.

As a starting point, by conducting transparent assessment on our work, we are modeling how we would like faculty to approach the assessment of teaching and learning. Most people find the prospect of open assessment to be intimidating, and faculty in particular often have valid concerns about how assessment data will be used (and by whom) for evaluative purposes. By demonstrating how assessment data can positively and constructively inform practice, we are leading the way for others to understand that such practices can be formative rather than punitive and that evidence-based practice can enhance the work that they do. And that same body of practice informs our backward design models for outcomes-based assessment, use of multiple sources of evidence to demonstrate effectiveness and development of empathy and constituent-focused goals; all processes that we frequently promote with our faculty, albeit in their context rather than ours.

Speaking of context, while the values of our profession, such as those mentioned in the previous paragraph, remain relatively stable, the vision of our role within our respective institutions continues to evolve (Gibbs, 2013). As we've mentioned several times in this volume, our vision of the field of educational development is expanding in terms of both scale, as we assert ourselves into larger change initiatives across our campuses, and scope, as we extend our thinking to include change processes that may take years, even decades, to be fully realized. This extension has several implications for our assessment practice. First, we might want to consider developing assessment plans with strategic outcomes that cover multiple years, including the articulation of stages and/or benchmarks along the way. Second, we might want to consider developing new outcomes, strategic goals, or methods intended to capture the sometimes elusive prey of cultural impact.

Figure 8.5. Excerpt from *Defining What Matters* (hub example).

Hub

"We make connections between people who would not otherwise be connected. We have a view into the university that's unique and can build on that to support initiatives and work towards cultural change."

Definition: In this capacity, CTLs serve as a forum, in the ancient Roman sense, as a place for exchange of ideas and where collaborative actions can occur. Actions that happen when CTLs play a hub role include adaptation, translation, redistribution, and cross-pollination—all of which reflect the importance of transcending disciplinary boundaries, elevating collective voices, including all voices, and amplifying voices typically unheard. Additionally, CTLs serve as hosts or facilitators of important institutional initiatives, which they may also lead or colead, and they highlight the work of others in the teaching and learning realm. Key values employed in this work are inclusion and collaboration. The institutional visibility of a CTL increases with this role, and the hub function has grown with the prevalence of campus-wide engagement in campus initiatives (e.g., diversity and inclusivity efforts, reforming general education, or STEM education).

Possible indicators to consider for documenting activity/achievement in this area:

In one year:

- In how many collaborations across campus, especially around key institutional initiatives, did your CTL engage?
- Are there documented instances of when a CTL disseminated examples of excellence in teaching and learning, so that they became more visible, or translated a project in one area to a parallel version adapted to another area?
- What networks were created when there was CTL involvement in projects that bring people together from different disciplines to work toward a common goal? How many cross-disciplinary teams or projects were developed in response to CTL programs?

Over several years:

- Are there increases in the number and extensiveness of collaborations between the CTL and other groups on campus? Do partners experience positive relationships, climate, and expectations (RCE) with the CTL (Greenwald & Zukoski, 2018)?

(Continues)

Figure 8.5. (*Continued*)

> - Is the CTL recognized as a "go-to" unit for convening diverse offices to work on a project or issue, as measured by the number requests that come *to* the CTL (even those that go beyond the boundaries of its scope and mission)?
> - Is there an increase in resources given to the CTL to advance its work over time (e.g., subawards from grants, FTE for assessment of collaborative initiatives)?

Source: Collins-Brown et al., (2018), *Defining What Matters: Guidelines for Comprehensive Center for Teaching and Learning (CTL) Evaluation*. Retrieved from www.podnetwork.org. Used with permission.

Organizational theorists have identified a learning organization as one in which learning permeates every aspect of how an enterprise does business. This may seem to be a self-evident quality for an institution of higher learning, but most researchers maintain that outside of their classrooms universities are (for the most part) not learning organizations, and some even question the degree to which it is possible for us to become one. To qualify as a learning organization, universities would have to foster what is called a *generative culture*, that is, a culture that responds nimbly and willingly to change, as opposed to getting mired in rigid bureaucratic procedures, and to the service of the greater good of the organization, as opposed to fulfilling individual or subgroup agendas. Some scholars and leaders have suggested that the cultivation of a campus-wide generative culture could be a long-term strategic goal for our profession (Condon et al., 2016), and if so, then this model may suggest indicators that could be assessed.

At least two of these indicators dovetail nicely with the values of educational development. The first is a high degree of cooperation and networking (you can read more about how to foster these yourself in chapter 9 of this volume), which fits well with the sociology of our field and its emphasis on networks on individual campuses and among practitioners (Greenwald & Zukoski, 2018). To translate this value into assessment, a group of educational developers created a comprehensive assessment guide based on a series of metaphors for the various organizational roles played by CTLs (e.g., hub, temple, incubator, and sieve). In the excerpt from the guide in Figure 8.5, you will see a description of the networking function (the hub), as well as some guiding questions and suggested indicators, both for short-term and long-term assessment. You are encouraged to consult the full version of the guide to explore assessment indicators and questions for the other sociological and cultural functions.

Another characteristic of a generative culture is a high degree of trust, sometimes referred to as social capital (Carpenter, Coughlin, Morgan, & Price, 2011). Trust can manifest itself in a number of ways, including collaboration; the propagation of shared norms and values; and an increase in risk-taking, innovation, and creativity. As educational developers, we want our faculty to feel free to talk about their teaching, including successes and failures, without fear of retribution, and we want to encourage them to invest their time and energy to try new things in their classrooms, even when we know that these experiments will not always work perfectly the first time. We can model this in our assessments by including narratives of our own successes and failures; documenting the long-term results of teaching transformation projects; indicating the ways in which we support faculty (or programs) who try innovative strategies; and generally demonstrating the transformative power of productive failure, whether in students, staff, or faculty. This body of evidence often takes the forms of anecdotes, stories, case studies, and testimonials. These kinds of narrative assessment can often prove to be more powerful than aggregate sources of data or evidence, but are, by their nature, limited in scale, scope, and replicability.

More broadly speaking, the cultural qualities described here (cooperation, trust, innovation) are much desired in and of higher education, but we academics have struggled to find effective ways to weave them into our historical culture. There are a handful of projects that rest on a foundation of trust and mutual cooperation among multiple institutions, including a growing interest in sharing open educational resources (OER). There are also a small number of national surveys that touch upon aspects of trust within a university, including COACHE, which measures faculty satisfaction, including transparency and consistency within the tenure and promotion process, and institutional climate surveys, which may include indicators of shared norms, especially in the areas of diversity and inclusion, but none that measure organizational culture directly. A few scholars have suggested that methods such as network analysis (interdependence) and text mining (implicit values) could generate new insights, but their potential is limited by the relatively sparse availability of larger data sets within higher education. Even outside of academia, there are only a handful of instruments and methods available to capture organizational culture (Jung et al., 2009; Scott, Mannion, Davies, & Marshall, 2003), and none seem to be fully compatible with the distinctively unconventional, varied, and intensive nature of academic life. The challenge of measuring cultural impact is truly at the frontier of our ongoing assessment efforts, and educational developers (such as yourself) have the potential to find themselves at the forefront of these conversations, whipping up new layers for our collective cake.

Speaking of that cake, one final principle to bear in mind is that it is all too easy to get consumed by assessment. Somewhat like teaching, assessment work will quickly fill up any space that you may choose to give it, so finding a balance between what you have to do, what you'd like to do, and what you can do is perhaps the best recipe for success. It is easy to read or hear about the extensive assessment work being done at large, well-established centers, including those that have in-house assessment experts, and, assuming you are not one of them, to feel inadequate and/or overwhelmed. If it should help, you are not alone, as this has happened, indeed sometimes continues to happen, to most of the authors of *Taking Flight*. You can always do more assessment than you are doing, so the trick is not to do as much as possible, but rather to try to do as much as you need, and that need includes spending time not only reporting but also deeply reflecting on your results. If you can do that, you'll find that your assessment isn't like Calvin's yo-yo—rather, it's a piece of cake.

Note

1. It should be noted that the American Council on Education (ACE) recently published a faculty development matrix that has emerged as a candidate for a common assessment rubric. You may consult their report at https://www.acenet.edu/news-room/Documents/The-Faculty-Development-Center-Matrix.pdf (Haras et al., 2019).

9

NETWORKING

Who Will You Work With?

The traditional view of how a university is organized is essentially hierarchical, with a president or chancellor at the top, extending downward through senior administrators, deans, department chairs, and faculty. In contemporary organizational theory, however, the emphasis has shifted away from such top-down or vertical models to understanding universities as horizontal systems, in which interconnected (and interdependent) networks of people, resources, and ideas all operate simultaneously. At the risk of using a somewhat dated metaphor, your goal is to become the Kevin Bacon of your campus.

As an educational development professional, you will want to consider ways to tap into these networks in order to advance your skills and reach your career goals. Unlike faculty, who work primarily through well-established departments (internally) and professional societies (externally), educational developers can often find themselves organizationally lonely, operating in what has been described as the liminal space between faculty and administration and outside of the conventional academic networks (Little & Green, 2012). In this field, it is often necessary to be proactive and intentional about building up your personal and professional networks.

As the representative of a particular organizational unit (e.g., a CTL), you will also take on responsibilities for networking on behalf of your center. This includes the identification, cultivation, and management of your own network of significant stakeholders, supporters, advocates, and power brokers, all drawn from multiple levels of the institution and beyond. These networks can serve to advance the success of your center, but, when utilized effectively, they can also serve to advance the teaching and learning culture of your institution more broadly (Poole, 2007).

Your Personal Network: Support Systems

In popular culture, networking seems to take place at country clubs or cocktail bars. While your well-used conference room or university cafeteria may not achieve such a high level of sophistication, the intent is the same: to become acquainted with people who can help you to succeed in your chosen career. The appearance of such naked ambition is often frowned upon in academia, but it is possible to engage in strategies for enhancing your personal network, especially if you are transitioning to a new role as an educational developer.

There are some tried- and- true methods for strengthening your personal networks, regardless of field. If you have not already done so, consider adding or updating your profile on social networking sites related to academia (e.g., www.academia.edu), joining relevant professional societies (e.g., the POD Network), subscribing or following significant journals and presses in the field (e.g., the *International Journal for Academic Development*), and signing up for alerts from funding agencies or databases. Because these sites can change often, we have provided an updated list of suggestions for online networks, professional societies, journals/presses, and funding/grant agencies specifically related to educational development, as part of the online materials available with the purchase of this book.

Another strategy for expanding your personal network is to engage in mentoring (Johnson, 2015). Mentoring is a well-researched subject with an established body of evidence-based practices that you are encouraged to consult, but there are considerations for mentoring that are specific to educational developers. In addition to being or having a mentor, you may also be asked to serve as a facilitator, someone who oversees mentoring programs for faculty or campus leaders; however, that function is largely independent of your personal network. If you do oversee mentoring programs, though, then you probably know that these often suffer from a shortage of qualified mentors. There are many reasons for this disparity, but one of the most prevalent in our field is the imposter syndrome, especially in the relative absence of formal credentials, including degrees (Rudenga & Gravett, 2019). You may find it difficult to believe that someone in your position, especially if you are new to the field, might have expertise to offer others. You may be pleasantly surprised to learn that you likely already engage in activities that are closely related to mentoring. Most educational developers, for example, provide confidential consultations or coaching sessions to individual or small groups of faculty on a regular basis, and this will shorten your leap to mentorship (Cruz & Rosemond, 2017; Little & Palmer, 2011).

Mentors offer advice not as a single consultation, but rather as part of a sustained relationship with mutually supportive goals. Engaging in such sustained relationships takes time and emotional investment in the success of another person, so choose the people you mentor carefully. Mentoring relationships vary widely, but if you want to plan how much time you can invest in these activities, approximately one to two hours of direct contact per month (usually during the academic year) might be considered a rule of thumb. It is common for educational developers to mentor students, staff, and faculty—sometimes simultaneously—so it can also help to be mindful of the respective calendars or time lines for each of these groups, for example, tenure and promotion deadlines, graduation dates, and major conferences. The emotional investment aspect should not be taken lightly either, as educational development is considered a form of emotional labor, perhaps more so than faculty or other administrative work, and you may find it necessary to pay more attention to how you manage your own emotional resources (Kowalik, Bostwick Faming, Fulmer, Donnell, & Smith, 2016).

Managing that balance may be a good topic of conversation between you and your own mentors, whom you should also choose carefully. The research on mentoring suggests that you should consider having multiple mentors, preferably at least one within your institution and one within your field. Finding the right mentor is often subjective and relies on interpersonal qualities that are difficult to generalize, but you can try focusing on people you admire and believe you can learn from as well as people who may be in a position to amplify your work and identify opportunities for recognition and/or advancement. Professional organizations, such as the POD Network or the Society for Teaching and Learning in Higher Education (STLHE), can be good sources for external mentors, and many provide targeted opportunities to connect with potential mentors at conferences or meetings.

In addition to formal mentors, you might want to consider identifying listening partners. These are people whom you can trust when you might need to express your feelings, including celebrations of your accomplishments, especially those minor or invisible victories that are difficult to share publically, as well as frustrations and disappointments that could be imprudent to share publically. Unlike mentoring relationships, listening partnerships are mutual. You each serve as the sounding board for the other, so you should expect to spend time listening as well as being listened to. Like mentors, it can be helpful to have listening partners inside and outside of your organization, particularly when the subject under discussion may be relevant to volatile internal politics or sensitive matters that require discretion.

If you are looking for personal networking opportunities with shorter time frames, you may be able to join or form communities of practice that extend your personal network (Stark & Smith, 2016). These small peer groups may be the product of shared experiences, such as those implemented in leadership development programs (whether campus or community based), or shared interests, such as interdisciplinary (e.g., STEAM) or multidisciplinary topics (e.g., assessment or first-year experiences). With functions similar to faculty learning communities, communities of practice serve to provide mutual support, accountability, and opportunities to learn from your peers, usually over the course of a semester or an academic year.

Your CTL's Network: The Tangled Webs We Weave

But enough about you. If you are reading this book, it is likely that part of your role is or will be network administrator for your center. This does not mean that you will be playing a role similar to an IT professional of the same name, of course, but it does mean that you bear responsibility for cultivating a network of relationships that supports the goals of your center. This is a complex and multifaceted task, but it is not uncommon for people to approach this task passively and allow networks to unfold organically. That being said, research and practice suggest that you can create more efficient and effective networks through intentional planning (Cross, Cross, & Parker, 2004; Cross, Liedtka, & Weiss, 2005; Kezar, 2014).

Identifying Your Stakeholders

The first step of planning your center's network focuses on identifying who your current and potential stakeholders are. While it may be relatively easy to identify those whom you serve (e.g., senior administrators) and whom you support (e.g., faculty) directly, your success will depend on extending the depth, breadth, and complexity of your networks. One possible strategy for extending your network is to consider the different facets of academic work.

Bolman and Gallos (2010), in their influential work titled *Reframing Academic Leadership*, identify the following ways of viewing, or framing, the work of universities: political, symbolic, structural, and human resources.

- In the *political frame*, a university is primarily viewed like a jungle or an arena, and its work is characterized as a competition for scarce resources.
- In the *symbolic frame*, a university is viewed as a theater or a temple, and its work is characterized by actions to make that work inspiring, important, or meaningful.

- In the *structural frame*, a university is viewed as a machine or factory, and its work is characterized as implementing efficient and effective processes and procedures.
- In the *human resources* frame, a university is primarily viewed as a family or clan, and its work is characterized as supporting the well-being and development of its members.

You can determine which of these frames characterize your own view of your work by taking the self-assessment provided by Bolman and Gallos, links to which are available at the website for this book.

Identifying particular stakeholders within your dominant frame may appear to be self-evident. Those who tend to view their work through a political frame, for example, would naturally identify senior leaders as well as potential competitors. However, we tend to overlook potential stakeholders that represent our less dominant frames. Bear in mind that while each of these frames provides a distinctive perspective, Bolman and Gallos (2010) emphasize that the frames are intended to be complementary and recommend that they work best together. That means that you can use their frameworks to identify different groups of stakeholders who support each of these perspectives or functions of a university, especially those stakeholders who provide frames that complement or supplement your own. The following sections present sets of guided questions designed to ensure that your list of stakeholders embraces all of these perspectives on how a university functions.

Identifying Stakeholders: Political Frame

- Who are your *senior leaders* with the most vested interest in your outcomes?
- Who are your *faculty leaders* with the most vested interest in your outcomes?
  Some examples may include the chair of your faculty senate, faculty union leaders, university committee chairs, or endowed professors.
- Who are the *external/community* partners with the most vested interest in your outcomes?
  These may include partners such as local businesses, nonprofit agencies, university alumni, retired faculty organizations or groups, K–12 schools or school districts, local or regional leadership programs, and others.
- Who are your primary *competitors* for resources (including funding and people)?
  These may include other units within your division or related divisions, such as colleges, in academic affairs.

Identifying Stakeholders: Symbolic Frame

- Who are your potential *allies*?

  These are campus or community stakeholders who share your vision for the teaching and learning community of your institution. Common allies include directors of service-learning, heads of general education programs or initiatives, research librarians, and educational technologists/instructional designers.

- Who are the campus *brokers*?

  These are campus or community leaders who hold particular influence, often informal, across your campus. In other words, these are the people to whom other people (especially faculty) listen—and so should you. Brokers are often individual faculty or staff members, so one of the best ways to identify them is to ask people who they listen to as part of informal conversations.

- Who are your *challengers*?

  These are campus or community stakeholders who might be presenting competing or conflicting visions of the teaching and learning community. Common potential challengers may include distance learning offices, IT security directors, student affairs administrators, and resistant faculty.

Identifying Stakeholders: Structural Frame

- Who are your *central connectors*?

  These are your "go-to" people who hold your network together. They are the people you go to for information or to find out what's happening. These are often staff members who are not in formal positions of authority, but whose knowledge and experience make them indispensable. Maybe there is a person on your campus, for example, whom everyone calls if they can't figure out how to fill out certain forms or to find vital information.

- Who are your *boundary spanners*?

  These are people who work across different units or departments within the university, often serving as a bridge between the two. In educational development, some of the most common boundary spanners work in educational technology (between IT and academic affairs) or student success (between academic and student affairs).

- Who are your *information brokers*?

  These are people who communicate within your center's network to keep everyone together and on the same page. In educational development, these are often faculty members who communicate the work of your center out to the broader campus, whether as faculty fellows or members of your advisory board.

- Who are your *peripheral specialists*?
  These are people on your campus who may not be part of your regular network, but on whom you can call when you need specialized support or knowledge. Examples may be advanced IT skills, the review of legal agreements or contracts, policies and procedures regarding space utilization, research compliance, or even deep disciplinary knowledge.

Identifying Stakeholders: Human Resources Frame

- Who are your *mentors*? These are the people you turn to for advice and counsel, often a senior leader or faculty member.
- Who are your *super fans*? These are faculty or staff who are the major supporters of the work of your center. They are likely to attend most of your events and encourage others to become involved.
- Who are your *resident experts*? These are faculty or staff who have developed expertise in faculty development and/or related pedagogical work independently from you and your center.
- Who are your *captive audience members*? These are faculty and staff who have reached a particular milestone or face a particular challenge for which your expertise may be needed, such as starting as new faculty, preparing a tenure file, or receiving poor student evaluations.
  [Note: For the purposes of listing your stakeholders, it may not always be possible to list individual names, but rather the name of the group, as may be appropriate for this category].

Mapping Your Stakeholders

After contemplating the preceding questions, we invite you to create a list of your stakeholders—that is, the people whom you will want to be part of your center's network. Once you've completed the initial list, step back and review what you've compiled.

Once you've finished and shared your list for comment with others, you may find that you have a considerable list of stakeholders, but try not to find the number daunting. This was only the warm-up, and we can turn to analyzing and prioritizing the people on your list.

Taking Flight Scenarios

You can practice applying what you've learned about networking and networking strategies in this chapter to the following case studies, drawn from common experiences of CTL directors:

The Grand Opening

You want to hold a grand opening celebration for your new or revitalized CTL. You have a budget for drinks and hors d'oeuvres for only about 100 people.

- Who has to be on your invitation list?
- Who should be on your invitation list?
- Who would you like to be on your invitation list?
- Who can you leave off your invitation list?

The Advisory Board

You have been tasked with creating an advisory board for your CTL. You are permitted to have 10 members serve on this body.

- Who do you ask for advice about these appointments?
- Who do you choose to be on your inaugural advisory board?
- Who approves your advisory board appointments?
- Who do you inform once the selections have been made?

The Project Team

You have been asked to lead a project to assess the impact of newly redesigned learning spaces on your campus. You have been given one academic year to produce a meaningful report and set of recommendations.

- Who do you include on your project team?
- How might you include other stakeholders outside of the project team? Who would those be?
- With whom would you consult about your recommendations?
- With whom would you share and communicate your results?

The first step is to analyze each of the stakeholders that you identified in Figure 9.1 and rank them according to three primary criteria: *contribution, willingness,* and *impact* on a scale of high, medium, or low.

> *Ask Yourself (and Others):*
> - Does this list focus on the relevant and important stakeholders who can work with you and your center right now? In the future?
> - Does the list appear to be balanced in terms of representation from different frames, areas of campus, and significant groups?
> - Is there anybody who should be added? Is there anybody who can be crossed off the list?

Contribution refers to what your stakeholder may have to offer to the success of your center, whether it is knowledge, access, counsel, expertise, or even legitimacy. In other words, this is (usually) the reason why they are a stakeholder in what you do. You would rank a stakeholder high in this category if his or her contribution to your work is critical for achieving one of your strategic goals.

Willingness refers to the degree to which your stakeholder is a willing participant in working with your center or, conversely, the degree of their reluctance, resistance, or inability to do so. You would rank a stakeholder high in this category if they are highly engaged, with little to no effort on your part to reach out or persuade them to do so.

Impact refers to the ability that the stakeholder has to influence or impact the work that your center does or, conversely, to impede your work if they are not included, represented, or taken into consideration. This influence may be either formal or informal. An example of a stakeholder who might be ranked high in this category would be a well-respected, long-term senior administrator who views faculty development as part of their responsibilities.

Now that you have ranked each stakeholder, create a stakeholder map. Using the matrix in Worksheet 9.1 (2, 3, and 4), map each of your stakeholders according to the three criteria previously listed, with contribution ploted on the y axis, willingness plotted on the x axis, and impact depicted by the size of the circle. When you're finished, you should have each of your stakeholders represented by a circle displayed across a collective grid.

Example: You have identified your first stakeholder, John Johnson, an associate dean in the College of Fine and Performing Arts, as MEDIUM contribution, HIGH willingness, and LOW impact. His circle might appear on your stakeholder map as depicted in Figure 9.1.

Example: You have identified your second stakeholder, Zheng Zhang, a senior faculty member in the College of Engineering with a campus-wide reputation for good teaching (a broker), as LOW contribution, MEDIUM willingness,

WORKSHEET 9.1
Stakeholder Map

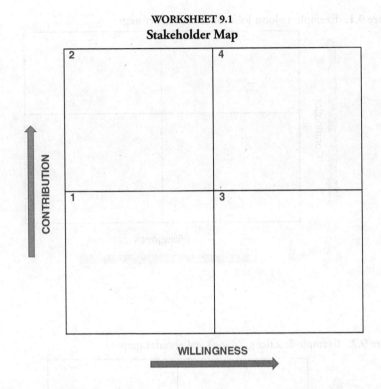

and HIGH impact. His circle might appear on your stakeholder map as depicted in Figure 9.2.

Example: You have identified your third stakeholder, Mavis Maples, director of multicultural affairs, as HIGH contribution, HIGH willingness, and MEDIUM impact. Her circle might appear on your stakeholder map as depicted in Figure 9.3.

Once you have completed your map, step back and look it over as a whole.

Ask Yourself:

- How strong is your understanding of your stakeholders—where are they coming from, what do they want, and what is their interest in your center? What else could you do to increase your understanding?
- What quadrants are the most crowded? The least? Where might there be opportunities to expand your list of stakeholders or to identify new potential stakeholders? Are there opportunities to limit your list of stakeholders and possibly remove some from your initial list?

Figure 9.1. Example 1: John Johnson's stakeholder map

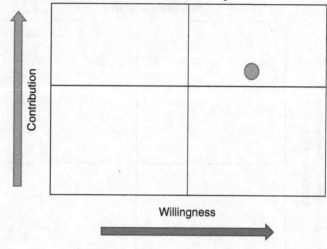

Figure 9.2. Example 2: Zheng Zhang's stakeholder map

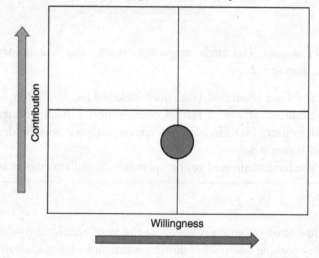

As an optional step, you may wish to look at the points of connection, overlap, or even conflict between your stakeholders and add these to your network map in the form of arrows, lines, circles, or other appropriate visual

Figure 9.3. Mavis Maple's stakeholder map

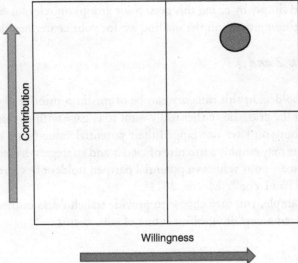

representations. This practice bears some resemblance to systems mapping (Chan-Hilton & Cruz, 2019), examples of which are provided for your inspiration in the multimedia package associated with this book.

Your Networking Plan

Now that you have mapped your stakeholders, the final step is to create a *networking plan*, which involves identifying tactics and/or strategies for engaging with your stakeholders. Don't worry, it is generally not feasible or desirable to engage a long list of stakeholders with a high level of intensity all the time (Baddache & Morris, 2011). Your networking plan is designed to help you prioritize your time and energy while maximizing your impact. We'll discuss networking plans quadrant by quadrant next.

Quadrant 1

The stakeholders in this category can be your lowest priority. You may only need to engage them tactically, that is, with short-term, semiplanned actions that primarily serve to inform, or simply keep them posted about what's happening (Baddache & Morris, 2011).

For example, you may choose to keep a stakeholder from this quadrant up to speed simply by cc'ing this person (or group) on relevant emails as they arise or including them on the mailing list for your center newsletter.

Quadrants 2 and 3

The stakeholders in this category can be of medium priority. Based on their position in the grid, they either really want to engage with you or have useful expertise, but you have not tapped their potential value (yet). Your engagement efforts may employ a mixture of tactics and strategies that communicate and underscore your value as a potential partner, holder of expertise, or agent of change (Baddache & Morris, 2011).

For example, you may choose to provide stakeholders in these quadrants with preferred access or visibility at one of your events.

Quadrant 4

These are your highest priority stakeholders, and you may want to create a separate plan in which you prioritize the strategic efforts you will make to engage and partner with each of them, both in the short-term and the long-term.

For example, you may choose to work with this person/unit/group on facilitating a major collaborative research project or grant, hosting a joint conference, or coleading a new campus initiative. If this person is a senior administrator, you may wish to identify strategic areas in which your center can add value to what they do or strategies for increasing your access.

Now that you've compiled a list of how you will engage with the people in your network, it's time to turn that list of action items into a plan, including an appropriate time line and means of accountability. In other words, it should include what you're going to do, when you're going to do it, how you will communicate what you're doing, and how you will know when you've completed the various steps successfully.

Based on our experiences, we suggest the following tips and tricks for developing your networking plan:

- Determine a plan that incorporates both short- (i.e., next semester) and long-term (i.e., five-year) goals, but leave room for revisiting your goals (especially the long-term ones) as the mission of your center evolves and responds to unforeseen changes in the campus climate.

- Take into account that turnover, especially in senior administrative positions, is likely to occur and consider delineating which aspects of your plan are person dependent and which are role dependent.
- Acknowledge that interpersonal engagement is both a talent and a skill, and not all staff members (including yourself) will be equally proficient in achieving the various tactics and strategies called for by your plan. While you can try to keep staff in their wheelhouses/comfort zones, it may also be an opportunity to strengthen their networking skills through professional development.
- Use visualization strategies. The idea of a network can take some time to wrap your head around, because it is highly conceptual and often challenges conventional ideas of how organizations function. It may be useful, for you or members of your team, to provide a visualization of the network you have built/are building. You can do this at the high end of the technology scale, using free or proprietary social network mapping software (e.g., Geffe or Centrifuge), or at the low end of the technology scale, using simple drawing tools and some well-placed sticky notes.
- Do what works best for you. These plans need not utilize a formal format—they are often intended for use primarily for you and/or your staff so you can use any means that works best for your team. Some centers use white boards or spreadsheets to monitor progress, while others may use visual tools, such as infographics. Note that while not official, networking plans can form the basis of more formal reporting and assessment efforts (see chapter 7).

The Campus Community: Getting a Seat at the Table

You and your center may have your own networks, but both of these are part of larger interconnected and interdependent systems of people, ideas, resources, and activities. Leaving external networks aside, contemporary organizational theory supposes that a university is composed not of a hierarchy of people in specified roles, but rather of variable, various, and varying networks. You—and your center—may not necessarily be the nexus or driver of these networks, but because of the multi- and transdisciplinary nature of our work, we often have a distinct advantage in our ability to see a wide variety of these networks across the campus (Williams et al., 2013). This means that you may have a leading role to play in monitoring and guiding these networks toward the transformation of your campus culture.

This organizational role is part of the shift in thinking about the role of CTLs. We no longer primarily see ourselves as providers of services or programs, but rather as "agents of change who build bridges across different functional, political, and anthropological divisions on their campuses" (Cruz, Cunningham, Smentkowski, & Steiner, 2018; Henderson et al., 2011; Schroeder, 2012). These bridges share a common vision of the campus as a teaching and learning community, with values that foster innovative teaching and effective student learning (Felten et al., 2007). These bridges can take the form of formal structures, such as the establishment of policy and procedures (e.g., faculty evaluation, general education, learning assessment), but also informal, grassroots, or behind-the-scenes connections (Cruz et al., 2018; Roxå & Martensson, 2009). In other words, we influence the culture and community of our campuses through our networks.

If we are to fully take on our role as agents of change, however, we also need to consider how we gain access to the spaces where critical conversations take place and to the people who are in a position to effect change most directly. In "The Role of Educational Developers in Institutional Change: From the Basement Office to the Front Office," Nancy Chism (1998) argues "If educational developers are isolated or nested within several layers of organizational structure so that we do not have direct communication with decision makers, our influence is curtailed" (p. 164). Her point is well taken: If we wish to enhance and reveal our impact, we must establish access points and occasionally forge pathways into decision-making circles. Occasionally, and often depending on your title (e.g., hired as an associate vice provost for faculty and educational development), an access point—a seat at the table—is provided. Ordinarily, it must be creatively negotiated.

This modern classic uses the imagery, and to a certain extent the literal proximity, of office space to discuss the elevation of educational development on campus and in higher education. While the title has haunted those of us who have operated highly successful CTLs from so-called garden-level spaces, the key principle is that we need entry points into decision-making circles if we wish to have the opportunity to be integrated into or to serve as a driver of institutional change. This argument is echoed in Connie Schroeder's (2012) influential book, *Coming in From the Margins: Faculty Development's Emerging Organizational Development Role in Institutional Change*, which drove many a director upstairs to negotiate a seat at the table. This proactive posture is important, especially on campuses where the potential of CTLs is not well established or understood. This entails exerting a certain amount of upward pressure, but it cannot come in the form of a hollow ask: You must bring something—concrete accomplishments or skills—to the table in order to earn a seat there. You should think about what compelling evidence you have so that *if* you have that seat, *then* you can have a greater impact, knowing that your currency is not how it will benefit your center, but how your center can advance the university through this decision.

While there is a temptation to run up the ladder, it is important to keep at least one foot planted firmly on the ground. It is reasonable to think that educational development is easier when you're in a front-office position, and frankly, sometimes it is—a little authority goes a long way. But peer credibility is critical. Leading from above *can* come at the expense of your base, and that's potentially a negative trade-off. As bell hooks (1990) noted, our position on the margins offers "the possibility of radical perspectives from which to see and create, to imagine alternatives, new worlds" (p. 207). We argue that this space—the margins—is not necessarily a negative place, state, or position that we should try to avoid, escape, or "come in from" but rather, as Emily Gravett and Lindsay Bernhagen (2015) argue, serve as a place we "choose to occupy" for its particular benefits, for "the margins can be valuable sites of knowledge production, highlighting the ways staff might contribute to organizational development."

What all of this amounts to is a series of strategic calculations and moves graphically represented in figure 9.4.

Figure 9.4. A Seat at the Table.

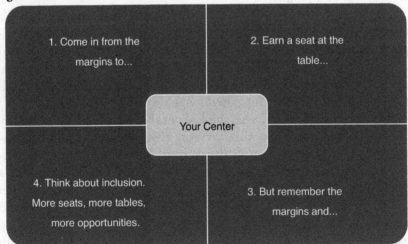

In "Negotiating a Seat at the Table," the authors argue that

> The desire to contribute more deeply to the institution's work on teaching
> and learning marks an "evolution in how we view our role as educational
> developers, both individually and collectively. It reflects a shift from think-
> ing about educational development as individual consultation with faculty
> clients to campus leadership as institutional agents of change. (Siering et
> al., 2015)

But as previously indicated (and in Worksheet 9.2), there's more than one
table; actually educational development involves multiple seats and multiple
tables, some of which are on the margins and some of which are ours to offer.

The following exercise is designed to help you determine where you
have, where you need, and to whom you should offer a seat at the table.
Use Worksheet 9.2 as a guide, filling in table names accordingly. Take it one
step further and consider who occupies which seats and maybe even draw
connections between them. And think about the seats you absolutely need,
those that you think should be permanent, and recognize that some may be
temporary. For each, think of the strategy associated with each move: If you
believe you need a seat at the deans' table, jot down how to get there. If you
think that a year's service on a committee would enhance your bond with
like-minded colleagues, how would you go about earning it and sustaining
the bond you forged during your appointment? With your own table, does
anyone—a faculty associate, for example—need to come on board (semi)
permanently to enhance your engagement and impact? Think further about
project-based seats and tables, knowing that while they may be temporary,
they may also be a priority.

Think about not only the number and kinds of seats you have but also
the number and kinds of tables you may have. Is there one for faculty development, another for service-learning, and another for supporting student
success, for example? In addition to strategically identifying seats and tables,
use this exercise to think about the work to be done there and how you will
orchestrate your CTL's participation through them.

As you conclude this exercise, think about the strategic partners and key
collaborators you can work with, knowing that like any healthy relationship we support one another. In the parlance of service-learning, it's ulti-
mately about mutuality: We give as much as we get, all in furtherance of a
greater good. Think about how discussions on diversity and inclusion can
be enriched through partnerships with your campus's office of diversity and
inclusion, its women's center, and related groups. Think about how learning
accessibility can be enriched through mutually beneficial relationships with

WORKSHEET 9.2
Seat at the Table Strategy

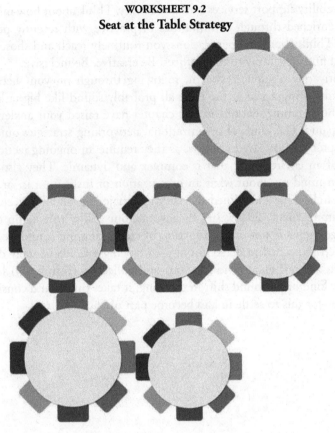

➤ Why aren't you there?

➤ How do we negotiate/earn/keep a seat at the table(s)?

➤ What about *our* table?

➤ How do we balance our faculty credibility and our administrative roles?

➤ Can our efforts on the margins earn us a seat at the "big" tables?

➤ Is it okay if we lose a seat at some tables?

Seat at the Table Strategy:

➤ Where do you think you most need to be?

your disability support services staff and library. Think about how mentoring can be enriched through communities of practice with recently promoted faculty. Think about the populations you routinely reach and those you do not, and find a pathway to their offices. Be creative. Be inclusive.

Cultivating a support system, following through on your networking plan, and getting a seat at the table all probably sound like big tasks. They are. If the recommendations in this chapter have raised your anxiety levels, do not panic. The kinds of organizational networking strategies outlined in this chapter are not easy to master, as they require an ongoing tactical navigation of an environment that is complex and dynamic. They also require a shift in mind-set about what an organization or institution is, or can be, and researchers have identified this shift as a major threshold concept in our field (Timmermans, 2014). In other words, our ability to take on our role as change agents is not only a function of cultivating the confidence, skills, and expertise needed to do so but also embracing a fundamentally different mind-set, at both an individual (you) and collective (your team) level. As with any kind of profound shift in thinking, it takes time—and considerable practice—for this to settle in and become part of your routine.

10

CONCLUSION

Where Are You Going to Go?

Susan Robison (2013) has a deceptively simple exercise in her book, *The Peak Performing Professor*, in which she asks readers (or participants in her workshops) to consider a scenario in which it is five years from the present day, and a phone is ringing nearby. Imagine, she suggests, that the phone call is coming from the person you had always hoped to hear from and they are asking you the question you most want to hear (Robison, 2013). Then comes the salient question: Who would be on the phone and what would they be asking, For many people, including several of the *Taking Flight* authors, the posing of this question produced startling results. Not because of the hidden aspirations it revealed, but because of the lack of them. We couldn't answer the question.

If you struggled with answering the question yourself, rest assured, you are (yet again) not alone. According to Robison, this response is not uncommon among academics, and there is research that suggests faculty in particular tend to struggle with long-term life planning, especially after tenure. While the reasons for this are not known, some have speculated that much of the trajectory of an academic career is laid out for you, following the established pathway from graduate school to assistant professor and so on through the ranks. This means that faculty have had few opportunities to practice setting long-term career goals for themselves. This challenge is compounded in a field such as ours, which takes place largely outside of traditional academic pathways. When educational developers meet for the first time, we often exchange origin stories, which explain how we entered into this field. More often than not, the decision seems to be unintentional, or at least not part of a concerted long-term plan. As much emphasis as we place on backward design models when working with faculty, it seems almost ironic that we are often less adept at applying these principles to ourselves.

You: A Five-Year Plan

If you come from a faculty background, you may be familiar with the idea of a five-year academic plan. For those who are not familiar with the concept, faculty work is often described as being a three-legged stool comprising research, teaching, and service, the order of importance of which varies by discipline and institution. This tripartite division is often reflected in evaluation processes, as faculty are asked to produce evidence of effectiveness in each of the three areas as part of tenure, promotion, and reappointment dossiers. Traditionally, the orientation of these dossiers has been primarily retrospective and their purpose primarily summative. This has begun to change, however, with the rising implementation of posttenure review, which has brought increased attention to the developmental stages of faculty careers (Austin, 2010; Brew & Boud, 1996; Gappa, Austin, & Trice, 2007). Administrative concerns over issues such as stalled associates (e.g., midcareer professors whose productivity appears to have plateaued) or disengaged late-career faculty (Baldwin, DeZure, Shaw, & Moretto, 2008; Huston, Norman, & Ambrose, 2007; Matthews, 2014; Zeig & Baldwin, 2013) have led to the integration of career coaching models, including the use of five-year plans, which are projected into the future and intended to facilitate sustained productivity across all three legs of the stool and throughout the course of a faculty member's career (Lieff, 2009).

It is an interesting thought experiment to consider how this process might transfer to a career in educational development (Harland & Staniforth, 2008). If you had to articulate your five-year career goals in teaching and learning, what could those look like? Many of us provide direct instruction, whether in the form of leading our own courses, supplementing other courses, or facilitating continuing education opportunities, but such roles are often peripheral to our primary job responsibilities. What could our version of a teaching portfolio look like? Our contribution to teaching and learning is primarily through service, by leading our CTLs, consulting with faculty, and serving on committees and participating in related activities. Perhaps our portfolio might include a delineation of our roles and responsibilities, as well as examples of resources and materials generated to support the work of others (see Table 10.1).

Similarly, educational developers are frequently called on to cultivate and apply expertise in teaching and learning, especially if we can direct that knowledge toward desired instructional outcomes. As service providers, we are expected to be proficient in a wide range of teaching approaches, theories, and research, but we often gather such knowledge on an as-needed basis.

TABLE 10.1
Teaching Dossiers and Educational Developer's Portfolios

Common Components	Teaching Dossier	Educational Developers Portfolio
1. Beliefs	**Teaching Philosopy**	**Educational Development Philosophy**
	Beliefs, philosophy, perspectives, and goals as a teacher	Beliefs, philosophy, perspectives, ethics, and goals as an educational developer that may also include elements of a teaching philosophy and leadership philosophy.
	What makes you unique or different from another teacher?	What makes you unique or different from another educational developer?
2. Actions	**Teaching Responsibilities**	**Educational Development Responsibilities**
a) Roles and Responsibilities	Summarize teaching roles, responsibilities, and experience	Summarize educational development roles, responsibilities, and experience.
	This may include teaching, mentoring, supervision, research into teaching in postsecondary education, teaching-related leadership, and any support of others in their teaching.	This may include teaching, mentoring, consultations, projects, supervision, research into teaching in postsecondary education, research into educational development, leadership responsibilities and/or aiding professional development of others related to teaching, learning, and institutional change.
	The focus tends to be primarily on helping students learn and improving your own teaching.	The focus is primarily on helping to improve teaching of others, the system and/or the teaching culture of an institution, in order to help improve student learning.
b) Course or Curriculum Development	Development of your own course or program. Experienced instructors may lead curriculum reform or new curricular development.	Development of courses and curricula to help others with sustained development of their teaching. Aiding others in developing their courses, programs, and curricula.

(Continues)

TABLE 10.1 (*CONTINUED*)

Common Components	Teaching Dossier	Educational Developers Portfolio
c) Service	Service related to teaching such as committees, action groups, policy development, curriculum redesign, discipline-based organizations supporting teaching within a particular field of study (e.g. engineering education)	Service related to educational development such as local committees, faculty and institutional level committees, provincial/state or national/international committees, action groups, policy development (may also include service related to teaching)
d) Personal Professional Development	Improving your own competency and knowledge in teaching in order to help student learning.	Improving your own competency and knowledge in educational development in order to help others develop their teaching or to help one's institution
3. Impact	Student and colleague feedback on teaching. Evidence of impact through teaching.	Student, participant, and colleague feedback on educational development. Evidence of impact through educational development (e.g., change in participation, change in structures, change in curriculum).
4. Future Directions	Usually future directions to develop as a teacher. It could include developing as an educational leader or senior administrator (e.g., faculty dean, vicepresident academic).	Usually future directions to develop as an educational developer, educational leader, change agent, centre director, or senor administrator (e.g., academic vice president or vice provost of teaching and learning).

Source: McDonald et al., 2016; used under Creative Commons license.

Some of us refer to this skill as educational development literacy, or, to put it more colloquially, how fast you can put your hands on what you need to become an instant expert on a subject when asked about it by a faculty member.

In addition to this broad arena, many of us identify a selected area (or two) in which we intend to develop much deeper knowledge. This can be easier said than done, however, as it can be difficult to commit to spending time on such goals when the day-to-day, immediate work has an incessant tendency to suck up all of our time (or maybe that's just us). By including professional learning goals in your five-year plan, you can build in a degree of commitment, accountability, and permission to set aside time to spend on activities such as reading relevant literature, perusing blogs or other social media, talking to experts, taking courses, obtaining certifications, attending conferencing, enrolling in massive open online courses, and engaging in similar activities (Kowalik et al., 2016). You could even think of this exercise as developing your personal curriculum, outlining what methods, strategies, and resources you are going to use to reach your mastery goals.

Ask Yourself:

Who might be calling you in five years to benefit from your pedagogical expertise or recognize your role as a thought leader? What steps will you begin to take to get there?

The components of a teaching portfolio are likely to be familiar to many of you, whether because you've created one for yourself or you work with faculty to develop theirs. There are also numerous books, articles, and guides to assembling the appropriate contents for an effective teaching portfolio (Costantino, De Lorenzo, & Kobrinski, 2002; Seldin, Miller, & Seldin, 2010). There are fewer guides when it comes to the presentation of research. The default option is often simply a bibliographic list of relevant artifacts, from published articles to successful grants, similar in format to a CV (or an academic resume), but that's for faculty. Like teaching, scholarship may be a peripheral aspect of our work. For many educational developers, contributions to scholarship are not directly rewarded or included in job responsibilities, but even then that doesn't mean that you won't find rich rewards to being an active scholar. Some educational developers continue to do research in their first discipline (if applicable), while others pursue research agendas related to teaching and learning; such as SoTL or related forms of educational research, often in collaboration with faculty or staff colleagues.

There is also the emerging field of the scholarship of educational development (SoED), in which we systematically analyze the work that we do through a variety of methodological and experimental lenses, as befits a field that draws practitioners from a multitude of disciplinary backgrounds (Amundsen & Wilson, 2012; Chism, Holley, & Harris, 2012; Clegg, 2012; Cruz, 2016; Felten et al., 2007; Knight, 2002; Little, 2013; M. Sweet et al., 2008). Like other forms of scholarship, SoED has its own journals (for an updated list, see the multimedia site associated with this book), leading questions and paradigms, and a recognized cadre of leading scholars. If you're curious about what SoED might look like, then you have to look no further, as *Taking Flight* is itself a synthesis of many SoED studies.

As a practicing educational developer, you have the advantage of already spending most of your time in our equivalent of a laboratory, which puts you on the front lines of developing new lines of scholarly inquiry and assessment. And SoED is intrinsically collaborative, which can connect you to colleagues at other institutions, even other countries. Not all SoED products take the form of published books and articles, either, as the provision of guides, digital artifacts, reports, supplementary resources, and other formats can also contribute to the field (just in case you were wondering, these resources include a number of guides and recorded workshops on how to develop a SoED project; Cruz, 2016; Cruz, 2017a; 2017b; Cruz & Reder, 2015). To put it more succinctly, if you'd like to continue, begin, or renew your role as a scholar, then your position as an educational developer affords multiple opportunities that can complement and enhance the work you do and the work we all do.

> *Ask Yourself:*
>
> Who might be calling you in five years to recognize your role as a leading scholar in our field? What steps could you take to begin developing your research agenda?

And there are other ways you can grow as a leader over the next five years and beyond. Throughout *Taking Flight*, we have emphasized how the field of educational development is in a period of profound transition as CTLs aspire to become more than just providers of discrete services. This means, too, that the work you do is more than just service (although that can be what draws many of us into the field), but also servant leadership. As we become more involved in organizational development, our skill set begins to overlap with that of senior administrators. There have been a number of studies of the pathways people take into our profession, but much work remains to be done on the pathways beyond it (Kahn, 2004). That being said, there is considerable anecdotal evidence and shining examples of educational developers moving into senior academic leadership positions, ranging from deans to provosts and chancellors. As faculty development becomes a more recognizable, and integral, part of an institution's overall success, the skills and expertise you develop at the CTL are increasingly likely to be applicable to broader leadership contexts.

Ask Yourself:

Would you like to receive a call in five years from a university offering you a position such as associate provost? If so, what kinds of skills, insights, and experience will you need to be able to do so successfully?

**TAKING FLIGHT SCENARIO: BECOMING A SCHOLAR
OF EDUCATIONAL DEVELOPMENT**

Imagine the following scenario: Students on your campus presented their demands to your administration and faculty, calling for an end to systematic and structural racism at your institution. In particular, they insist on a curriculum that reflects diverse perspectives and classrooms that are inclusive learning spaces. As a result, you are hearing from faculty who want to know how to respond with revised syllabi, and you are also hearing (sometimes from students) of instances of microaggression and tokenizing of students of color in classes. You're responding to each request with the materials you have and some just-in-time research on strategies, but you know there is— or must be —a growing body of research on these topics out there.

Now, let's see if we can generate a research question based on this case.

Here are some of our ideas:

- How can we synthesize the research on inclusive teaching and learning in a way that would effectively serve the stakeholders on your campus?
- What are timely and effective modes of faculty development for issues of diversity and inclusion?
- How do faculty perceptions of issues of diversity and inclusion compare to those of students? Where are the gaps?

Now it's your turn to draw on your background, expertise and interests.

What research question(s) come to mind for this case?

What are some possible methodologies or approaches for pursuing your research question in this case?

What are some possible assessments or measures for studying your research question in this case?

Now, consider a scenario you have faced, or expect to face, in your own work and look at through the lens of scholarship. What would happen if you ask yourself the same questions, using your own real-life scenario as the focus?

Source: B. Smentkowski, used by permission of the author.

Leadership takes many shapes and forms, however, and you don't have to move up or outside of your center in order to think about how you might want to grow your influence. If your CTL (or campus) provides opportunities for leadership development, such as academies or short courses, you will know that there are seemingly innumerable typologies, taxonomies, and assessments of leadership styles and approaches (Cruz & Rosemond, 2017). We've already covered thought leadership, intellectual or scholarly leadership, servant leadership, and administrative leadership, but educational developers are often attracted to less formal roles that don't always show up in the literature, especially those that require skills in brokering solutions or managing the flow of people and ideas. You may find that you can be a very effective agent of change largely behind the scenes, by taking advantage of your careful cultivation of informal networks, strong relationships, and deep knowledge of campus cultural norms (Roxå & Martensson, 2009; Williams et al., 2013).

Ask Yourself:
When they call you in 5 (or even 20) years to recognize you for your leadership contribution, what sort of impact would you like to have had? What difference do you aspire to make?

Ask Yourself:
What would you like your portfolio to look like in five years? What elements will make it distinctly your own?

As educational developers, our five-year plans may bear some resemblance to those of a faculty member or an administrator, but they are likely to also reflect the distinctive organizational space that we occupy, working as we do in spaces between the more formal structures of a traditional university (Dawson, Britnell, & Hitchcock, 2010; Harland & Staniforth, 2008). If you look at the suggested elements of an educational developer's professional portfolio (Table 10.2), you may notice that the elements include a marriage of elements from faculty and administrative positions, but a few categories or areas of emphasis are uniquely ours.

Your CTL: A Five-Year Plan

Imagine that we slightly reframe Robison's (2013) phone call exercise to be directed not at an individual person, but to your CTL as a unit. A CTL is

TABLE 10.2
Elements of the Educational Developer's Portfolio

Philosophy	Approaches, Methods, and Materials
Roles and Responsibilities	Effectiveness and Impact
Teaching	Innovations and Leadership
Scholarship	Projects and Collaborations
Professional Development	Effectiveness and Impact

Source: Adapted from McDonald et al., 2016, with reference to W. A. Wright and Miller, 2000.

not just an amalgamation of the person or people who work there. It has a distinct identity and, some might say, personality. As a tangible space, your CTL serves a strong symbolic function. It serves as a safe space for faculty, not only those who are struggling but also those who are daring. It serves as the physical embodiment of the significance you place on the teaching and learning mission of your institution (Cruz, 2018). It shows to your faculty, your staff, your alumni, and your community that you are committed, as an institution, to doing everything you can to support your faculty so that they can teach your students well. In five years, who will we want to call our CTL's main line and what would they be asking of you?

In some ways, this may be an easier question to answer than the first because you've already spent time considering your response—that is, at least in part, what the strategic planning process is designed to do. Your strategic plan functions similarly to your professional portfolio; it is the portfolio for your CTL. To that end, you will have multiple components and versions of your strategic plan. Some people believe that the short version, such as you might have on your web page (for an example, see the University of Pittsburgh's model in chapter 5), is the final product, but you will most likely be tasked with creating a fairly hefty binder that provides a cogent summary of the activities you have taken to get you to the final statement of vision, mission, and goals.

One of our former chancellors once remarked that the purpose of a strategic plan was to sit on a shelf and gather dust. The quote was often cited by cynical faculty, but it was, in fact, taken out of context. The chancellor went on to say that the most important aspect of the strategic plan was not the hefty binder that came out at the end. Rather, he believed that the value in strategic planning lay in the process, of getting different stakeholders to talk to each other, to look outside of our day-to-day work and toward the future, to set intentional goals, and to transmit values and institutional identity. In other words, rather than viewing the construction of a document such as

TABLE 10.3
Components of a CTL Strategic Plan

The following are the key elements of our strategic plan. They are offered as examples, not as a formula.

Elements	Description
Executive Summary	Provides at-a-glance highlights from our strategic plan
Introduction	Documents the Center's vision, mission, and core values and commitments
Environmental Scan	Considers several facets of context for the work we do in our Center, including aspects of university context (results from our Instructional Needs Assessment and key institution-level priorities and intiatives that have a bearing on our work) and of national/global context (trends in higher education and in faculty and instructional development). Also includes a discussion of the increasing demand for our services and of the larger market for recruiting and retaining qualified, credible staff.
SWOT Analysis	Describes the Center's "current state," with attention to SWOT activities and the results from our regular Service Quality Survey. Subsections include discussion of ways to builf on strengths and seize opportunities and to overcome weaknesses and mitigate threats.
Benchmarking	Describes our approach to benchmarking, key benchmarking characteristics, and
Goals and Measures	Articulates strategic directions and goals, with concrete year-by-year measures for the specific ways we will achieve those goals and performance goals by team
Tracking and Assessment	Lays out a plan for regular checks for progress and opportunities for adjustment
Resources Needed	Explains resources needed to achieve vision and goals
Appendix	Provides supplementary documents, including a lsit of resources consulted

Source: Lohe, 2012. Used with permission of the author.

this as a chore; consider each component as an opportunity to engage with a wider variety of potential constituents and stakeholders.

That engagement with stakeholders and constituents is the cornerstone of our emphasis on *responsiveness*, one of the four *R*s that define our

Enhancing your CTL's visibility, presence, reputation, credibility and impact.

On campus visibility can be enhanced through. . .

- Dynamic and responsive programming (workshops and institutes)
- Campus-wide events, conversations, conferences, and celebrations of faculty success
- Novel innovations of your staff, your faculty, and in your programming

A ubiquitous positive presence can be established through. . .

- Flyers and posters for center-sponsored events
- Posters for faculty accomplishments, including (collaborative) research
- Internal journals and publications
- Gathering, archiving, and sharing evidence-based practices from faculty
- An updated and visually engaging web presence
- Exhibiting expertise in your academic field *and* your administrative role
- Newsletters
- "What I do" business cards and "who we are, what we do" flyers, inserts, etc.
- Expertly visualized data

Our reputation can be enhanced through. . .

- Initiatives and opportunities that require your individual and CTL's expertise
- Amplifying faculty success/completion/accomplishment in:
  - SoTL
  - Course (re)design
  - Learning communities
  - Educational technology
  - Grants
  - Student success-oriented faculty development
  - Peer observation of instruction and SGIDs

Our impact can be revealed through the written word in. . .

- Annual/semesterly/quarterly reports
- White papers
- Newsletters
- Leadership on institutional initiatives
- Strategic plans

Our credibility can be enhanced through active engagement beyond campus...

- Scholarship (in both fields)
- Conference activity (in both fields)
- Continuing professional/leadership development
- Editorial service
- Progressive engagement in the field and with other institutions

profession (M. C. Wright et al., 2018). Being responsive is not simply responding to inquiries efficiently and effectively, but also making your efforts visible across campus. There are many benefits to having people know where you want to be in five years and how that vision was shaped by their needs. This is not just an exercise in self-promotion. Rather, communicating your goals increases your presence, which, in turn, enhances your reputation, which then supports your credibility, and then gets you to more seats at more tables and further advances the impact you can have on your campus.

Ask Yourself:

- In five years, who do you want to know about the work that your CTL is doing?
- Where and how do you want your presence to be known?
- Who might be calling you (rather than you calling them) to be a part of a major campus initiative, to be a member of a campus think tank, or to be recognized for your role in fostering the campus teaching and learning community?

You may find that your aspirations run deeper, however, than can be captured in an official document or formal award. Another one of our "*R*" pillars is our *relational abilities*, or how we nurture a wide variety of relationships, and these are not always individual one-to-one relationships, but rather how your CTL builds its collective network (M.C. Wright et al., 2018). Your ability to leverage your relationships may originate in your formal programs, such as new faculty orientation, faculty learning communities, or intensive academies/institutes, but enhanced relationships can also be the product of events that serve a social purpose, such as receptions, happy hours, lunch programs, or even just informal meetings, such as sharing a cup of coffee. As host or hostess, you can call on your relational skills to not just make your own relationships but to facilitate relationship building beyond the CTL by taking the opportunity to steer people toward one another, find common ground, share information, and start conversations about shared interests. Although the benefits of these kinds of activities can be difficult to capture tangibly, many experienced educational developers report that they find them to be among the most effective change strategies they have at their disposal.

Ask Yourself:

In five years, what aspects of campus culture would you most like to see changed; and how can you build relationships to facilitate that change?

TAKING FLIGHT SCENARIO:

Over the past three months, you have talked to faculty (four, each from a different discipline) who have mentioned that there appears to be an increase in students who are choosing to withdraw from group work. From what they've shared, it wouldn't appear to be a flood of students, but a few more in each class when compared to previous iterations of the same course.

What, if anything, would you do in response to this observation? Jot down your response *before* reading the response options listed next.

_____

_____

_____

Response Options:

A. Consult with these faculty individually and work together to generate strategies for promoting more engagement in group work and/or finding meaningful alternative assignments for those students who choose not to participate.

B. Create a common resource (e.g., handout, web page) for faculty facing similar problems, including relevant research on potential causes, as well as some strategies for navigating the situation.

C. Offer a workshop on the subject, or add a feature on the subject to an existing event or program, such as new faculty orientation or your annual teaching institute or possibly the focus of a book group or learning community.

D. Collaborate with the faculty members who brought this to your attention to conduct assessments of their interventions to address the issue and publish the results. Recognize and reward their efforts, including providing some publicity for their results.

E. Encourage the student leadership office to partner with departments/programs to sponsor student events designed to enhance social intelligence (e.g., etiquette dinner for social skills).

F. Reach out to those programs or departments that integrate group work in many of their classes/for many of their students and investigate how widespread the issue seems to be .Connect your findings to research literature and reports from other institutions.

G. Partner with your office of institutional effectiveness (or similar) to develop/adapt an assessment that may capture the characteristics, features, or contributing causes of social isolation/lessening of social skills, Conduct a campus-wide study and share your results and recommendations across campus.

H. Invite representatives from student affairs, counseling, residential living, psychology, sociology, first-year experiences, service-learning, athletics, ROTC, and others to a summit in which you discuss strategies for strengthening students' social skills at the curricular, cocurricular, and extracurricular levels.

I. Draft (with subcommittee of group from option H) new campus policy to identify students whose social skills may put them at risk. Include new course designation for those courses that integrate a high degree of team/group work or other forms of sustained collaboration.

J. Propose (with group) to your provost and the council of deans that increasing social skills be made a priority on campus and the focus of an integrated, five-year campaign that includes course redesign incentives, student programs, intensive marketing, and partnerships with local businesses that rely on effective teamwork.

K. Go to the hot new restaurant downtown and have a drink and some tapas with the assistant vice president for student affairs, the men's soccer coach, and a member of the faculty senate (also your friends). Talk about what you've been seeing. Pitch some ideas about what they could do, and why doing it would make them look good.

L. Start talking about the issue everywhere you go. Mention it in meetings. Talk about it over lunch. Bring it up when you consult with faculty and ask them about it. Talk to your students and student workers. Drop a reference to it when introducing a speaker. Introduce faculty who share the problem to each other. Start conversations.

What do you notice about the changes in the responses as the move from A to L? What patterns do you see?

Of the response options given, which would you predict would be the most effective?

Of the response options given, which do you think would be the easiest for you to achieve? The most difficult?

Source: L. Cruz, D. Lohe, & M. Palmer, 2017. Used with permission of the authors.

One social science concept that has been used to articulate the value of building relationships is *social capital,* defined as the investment you put into relationships and how that investment pays off in benefits. Social capital can be seen as an individual quality, such as the degree to which you can utilize the people in your personal network to advance your career. It can also be collective. If you are a director, managing the social capital of your center wisely can be a significant responsibility that entails not only being able to call upon the stakeholders in your network but also knowing the levels of accumulated capital you have achieved. To put this another way, it can be quite helpful to have a working knowledge of who "owes" you favors (and to whom you owe), whom you can count on for certain tasks, whom you may have called on too often, and whose judgment or expertise you can trust (and whose you can't). For most theorists, though, social capital is about the value of larger scale social networks, such as those that characterize a university, and how these serve to enhance collective qualities such as trust, reciprocity, innovation, and a sense of belonging to the benefit of everyone (Adler & Kwon, 2002; Carpenter et al., 2011; Liebowiz, 2007).

Ask Yourself:

What could you be doing to increase the social capital on your campus over the long run?

Your responsiveness and relational abilities also contribute to your effectiveness as an advocate for *resources* (our third *R*). We tend to view resources primarily as restraints, but they are also your building blocks, and advocating for resources affords you more opportunities to reinforce your value in front of different audiences. The key verb here is advocating, and the skill of advocacy is distinct from those more familiar to our profession, such as coaching, developing, facilitating, or educating. In a sense, we are not asking for resources, but rather persuading an audience of the value of what those resources would enable us to do. This entails a shift from thinking of how we fund programs or people to how we make a vision take flight.

In our earlier form as support centers, CTLs often evoked a consciously impartial stand when it came to divisive or sensitive matters. Cloaked in our confidentiality polities, we adopted a stance of neutrality and treated our CTL spaces as Switzerland. Former POD president William Bergquist once noted, too, that we had a tendency to "cool the mark" or diffuse conflict through building consensus and finding common ground. This is becoming less the case, as the field of educational development takes on a stronger advocacy role, whether in bringing our collective knowledge of the faculty to the table or providing experience and expertise drawn from the growing body of best practices in teaching and leading. The publication of *POD Speaks* is itself evidence of the emerging role at the national level, but you can also be a significant, dedicated, and high-level voice on your campus that is dedicated to strengthening the teaching and learning aspects of your mission.

Ask Yourself:

- Over the course of the next five years, what kinds of issues do you think will be worth advocating for?
- What challenges should we be preparing to face down the road?
- What are the places where you'd like to speak up and have your collective voice heard?

Taking Flight Tip: The Check-In

Several of your *Taking Flight* authors use a quick guided inquiry exercise, such as in Box 10.1, to periodically check in (or is it check up?) on where the CTL is headed. The exercise works well as either an individual or team exercise.

BOX 10.1.
Check-In Prompts to Help You Take Flight

Address/complete each of the following prompts in two sentences. Don't spend more than five minutes total on all the prompts. Go!

Role: Self and Center

My role as _____ *is to:*

The role of my center is to:

Priorities: Own and Other

Actual: My top three priorities are:

1.
2.
3.

BOX 10.1. (*CONTINUED*)

Perceptual: My top three priorities under new leadership or based on external input are:

1.
2.
3.

Actual: The top three priorities for my center (in my opinion) are:

1.
2.
3.

Perceptual: The top three priorities of my center (according to others) are:

1.
2.
3.

Culture Change

Evidence of my impact can be found/seen in:

Evidence of my center's impact on campus culture/the institutional ethos is found in:

My center can have a greater impact on campus culture and institutional effectiveness if:

Goals

Briefly identify 4–5 tangible goals the center should target/seek to accomplish this year:

Educational Development: A Five-Year Plan

Those of you who are detail oriented may have noticed that the previous section covered only three of the Rs billed as the four pillars of our work. The final pillar, *research*, is the closest word that starts with an *R* that reflects our commitment to evidence-based practice. This phrasing is very intentionally differentiated from the rhetoric of best practices, the latter of which tend to be static, while the former are more dynamic. The evidence base for our work is constantly not only growing but also expanding in both depth and breadth. In the scholarship of educational development, we are moving away from an emphasis on the assessment of practice and toward a richer theoretical, conceptual, and empirical base (Haras et al., 2017; Hutchings, 2007; Macfayden et al., 2017; Springborg & Horri, 2016). Recent breakthroughs in the learning sciences have been astonishing and, at times, game changing as what we thought we knew about teaching or learning gets overturned in favor of new insights or revelations.

Where will the field of educational development be in 5 years? Or 10? Or 20? On one hand, we simply can't predict the future. There is no educational development equivalent of a crystal ball, tea leaves, or Greek oracles. On the other hand, we can use our in-depth knowledge of teaching and learning to anticipate what might lie on the road ahead and to work to prepare ourselves for what may be coming down the pike. To do so involves another shift in mind-set, from reactive to proactive. Reactive is not the same as responsive; the shift means that you may be responding to implicit or future needs rather than those that are right in front of you. The cycle of innovation works similarly to the Taking Flight life cycle, in that our projects and programs will be created, but then they will also need to be retired and replaced, by which time we will already (hopefully) have built their replacements (Chan-Hilton & Cruz, 2018, 2019).

And that cycle of innovation may apply to not only our scholarship and practice but also our field more broadly. We got our start as a bridge between research and practice, inextricably entwined with a deep, even idealistic, belief in the transformative power of teaching, whether as an art, a craft, a skill, or a science (Grant et al., 2009; Lee & McWilliam, 2008). That spark of idealism remains, but it has now itself become transformed as we harness its symbolic power to make deeper and deeper inroads into sustained and sustainable cultural change, not only on our respective campuses but also, dare we say it, across higher education itself. We may currently be enmeshed in our so-called age of accountability, but we can also be building toward what we want the next chapter of our story to become. We are all so fortunate to be part of a dynamic field at a pivotal moment in its history, one that affords us incredible opportunities to shape where it will go in the future. Let us all take flight.

REFERENCES

Adler, P. S., & Kwon, S. W. (2002). Social capital: Prospects for a new concept. *Academy of Management Review, 27*(1), 17–40.

Allingham, M. (2002). *Choice theory: A very short introduction.* Oxford, UK: Oxford University Press.

Ambrosino, R., & Peel, J. (2011). Faculty development programs: Assess the impact on instructional practices, and student learning and motivation. *Journal of Faculty Development, 25*(2), 33–38.

American Council on Education (2017). *Institutional commitment to teaching excellence: Assessing the impacts and outcomes of faculty development.* Retrieved from http://www.acenet.edu/news-room/Documents/Institutional-Commitment-to-Teaching-Excellence.pdf

Amundsen, C., & Wilson, M. (2012). Are we asking the right questions? A conceptual review of the educational development literature in higher education. *Review of Educational Research, 82*(1), 90–126.

ASQ Service Quality Division (2016, May). *Strengths, opportunities, aspirations, results (SOAR) analysis.* Retrieved from http://asqservicequality.org/glossary/strengths-opportunities-aspirations-results-soar-analysis/

Austin, A. (2002). Preparing the next generation of faculty: Graduate school as socialization to the academic career. *The Journal of Higher Education, 73*(1), 94–122.

Austin, A. E. (2010). Supporting faculty members across their careers. In K. J. Gillespie & D. L. Robertson (Eds.), *A guide to faculty development* (2nd ed., pp. 363–378). San Francisco, CA: Jossey-Bass.

Austin, A. E., Sorcinelli, M. D., & McDaniels, M. (2007). Understanding new faculty background, aspirations, challenges, and growth. In R. P. Perry & J. C. Smart (Eds.), *The scholarship of teaching and learning in higher education: an evidence-based perspective* (pp. 39–91). Dordrecht, The Netherlands: Springer.

Baddache, F. & Morris, J. (2011). *BSR's five-step approach to stakeholder engagement.* New York, NY: Business for Social Responsibility (BSR). Retrieved from https://www.bsr.org/en/our-insights/report-view/bsrs-five-step-approach-to-stakeholder-engagement

Baldwin, R., DeZure, D., Shaw, A., & Moretto, K. (2008). Mapping the terrain of mid-career faculty at a research university: Implications for faculty and academic leaders. *Change: The Magazine of Higher Learning, 40*(5), 46–55.

Baran, E. (2016). Investigating faculty technology mentoring as a university-wide professional development model. *Journal of Computing in Higher Education, 28*(1), 45–71. Retrieved from https://search-proquest-com.liblink.uncw.edu/docview/1826525534?accountid=14606

Bataille, G., & Brown, B. (2006). *Faculty career paths: Multiple routes to academic success and satisfaction.* Westport, CT: Praeger.

Beach, A. L., Sorcinelli, M. D., Austin, A. E., & Rivard, J. K. (2016). *Faculty development in the age of evidence: Current practices, future imperatives.* Sterling, VA: Stylus.

Behar-Horenstein, L. S., Garvan, C. W., Catalanotto, F. A., & Hudson-Vassell, C. N. (2014). The role of needs assessment for faculty development initiatives. *Journal of Faculty Development, 28*(2), 75–86.

Belanger, C., Belisle, M., & Bernatches, P.-A. (2011). A study of the impact of services of a university teaching centre on teaching practice: Changes and conditions. *Journal on Centers for Teaching and Learning, 3,* 131–165.

Berlin, I., & Hardy, H. (2013). *The Hedgehog and the Fox.* Princeton University Press.

Bernhagen, L., & Gravett, E. (2017). Educational development as pink collar labor: Implications and recommendations. *To Improve the Academy, 36*(1), 9–19.

Bolman, L. G., & Gallos, J. V. (2010). *Reframing academic leadership.* Hoboken, NJ: Wiley.

Boman, J., Yeo, M., & Matus, T. (2013). Support for new faculty members: What do they perceive they need? *Collected Essays on Learning and Teaching, 6,* 13–17. Retrieved from https://search-proquest-com.liblink.uncw.edu/docview/1697505014?accountid=14606

Bond, R. M., Fariss, C. J., Jones, J. J., Kramer, A. D. I., Marlow, C., Settle, J. E., & Fowler, J. H. (2012). A 61-million-person experiment in social influence and political mobilization. *Nature, 489,* 295–298.

Bowen, J. A. (2012). *Teaching naked: How moving technology out of your college classroom will improve student learning.* San Francisco, CA: John Wiley & Sons.

Boyer, R. K. (2016, July 18). Achieving a culture of communication on campus. *Chronical of Higher Education.* Retrieved from https://www.chronicle.com/article/Achieving-a-Culture-of/237120

Brew, A., & Boud, D. (1996). Preparing for new academic roles: A holistic approach to development. *The International Journal for Academic Development, 1*(2), 17–25.

Brinthaupt, T., Cruz, L., Otto, S., & Pinter, M. (2019). A framework for the strategic leveraging of outside resources to enhance CTL effectiveness. *To Improve the Academy, 38*(1), 82–94.

Brooks, D. C., March, L., Wilcox, K., & Cohen, B. (2011, September). Beyond satisfaction: Toward an outcomes-based, procedural model of faculty development program evaluation. *Journal of Faculty Development, 25*(3), 5–12.

Brown, P. C., Roediger III, H. L., & McDaniel, M. A. (2014). *Make it stick: The science of successful learning.* Cambridge, MA: Harvard University Press.

Capela, S., & Brooks-Saunders, A. (n.d.). *A different approach to strategic planning: SOAR-building strengths-based strategy.* Retrieved from coanet.org/conference/ppt/A7Presentation.pdf

Carpenter, A. N., Coughlin, L., Morgan, S., & Price, C. (2011). Social capital and the campus community. *To Improve the Academy, 29*(1), 201–215.

Chalmers, D., & Gardiner, D. (2015). An evaluation framework for identifying the effectiveness and impact of academic teacher development programmes. *Studies in Educational Evaluation, 46,* 81–91.

Chan-Hilton, A. & Cruz, L. (2019). Crossing the streams: Improvement science, educational development, and systems theory in higher education. In R. Crow, B. N. Hinnant-Crawford, & D. T. Spaulding (Eds.), *The educational leader's guide to improvement science: Data, design and cases for reflection.* Gorham, ME: Myers Education Press.

Chan-Hilton, A., & Cruz, L. (2018, August 6). *Jumping the s-curve: A systems thinking toolkit for educational developers.* Presentation given to the International Consortium of Educational Development, Atlanta, GA.

Chism, N. (1998). The role of educational developers in institutional change: From the basement office to the front office. *To Improve the Academy, 17,* 141–154.

Chism, N., Gosling, D., & Sorcinelli, M. D. (2010). International faculty development: Pursuing work with colleagues around the world. In K. J. Gillespie & D. L. Robertson (Eds.), *A guide to faculty development* (2nd ed, pp. 243–258). San Francisco, CA: Jossey-Bass.

Chism, N., & Szabó, B. (1997). How faculty development programs evaluate their services. *Journal of Staff, Program, and Organization Development, 15*(2), 55–62.

Chism, N. V. N., Holley, M., & Harris, C. J. (2012). Researching the impact of educational development: Basis for informed practice. *To Improve the Academy, 31*(1), 129–145.

Chrystall, F. H., & Lohe, D. (2015, June 16–19). *Strategic planning.* Presentation given at the Institute for New Faculty Developers, Asheville, NC.

Cialdini, R. B., Demain, L. J., Sagarin, B. J., Barrett, D. W., Rhoads, K. & Winter, P. L. (2006). Managing social norms for persuasive impact. *Social Influence, 1*(1), 3–15.

Cilliers, F. J., & Tekian, A. (2016). Effective faculty development in an institutional context: Designing for transfer. *Journal of Graduate Medical Education, 8*(2), 145–149.

Clegg, S. (2012). Conceptualising higher education research and/or academic development as 'fields': A critical analysis. *Higher Education Research & Development, 31*(5), 667–678.

Cohen, M.W. (2010). Listen, learn, and lead: Getting started in faculty development. In K. J. Gillespie & D. L. Robertson, (Eds.), *A guide to faculty development* (2nd ed., pp. 67–82). San Francisco, CA: Jossey-Bass.

Collins, J. (2001). *Good to great: Why some companies make the leap . . . and others don't.* New York, NY: HarperCollins.

Collins, J. (2005). *Good to great and the social sectors: Why business thinking is not the answer.* New York, NY: HarperCollins.

Collins, R. (2010). *A graphical method for exploring the business environment.* Reading, UK: Henley Business School. Retrieved from http://users.ox.ac.uk/~kell0956/docs/PESTLEWeb.pdf

Collins-Brown, E., Cruz, L., Torosyan, R. (2016). *The 2016 POD Network membership survey: Past, present, and future.* POD Network. Retrieved from https://podnetwork.org/content/uploads/2016podmembershipreportprintnomarks.pdf

Collins-Brown, E. (2018). *Defining What Matters: Guidelines for Comprehensive Center for Teaching and Learning (CTL) Evaluation.* POD Network. Retrieved from https://podnetwork.org/content/uploads/POD_CTL_Evaluation_Guidelines __2018_.pdf

Condon, W., Iverson, E. R., Manduca, C. A., & Rutz, C. (2016). *Faculty development and student learning: Assessing the connections.* Bloomington, IN: Indiana University Press.

Connolly, M. R., Savoy, J. N., Lee, Y.-G., & Hill, L. B. (2016). *Building a better future STEM faculty: How doctoral teaching programs can improve undergraduate education.* Madison, WI: Wisconsin Center for Education Research, University of Wisconsin-Madison.

Cook, C., & Kaplan, M. (2011). *Advancing the culture of teaching on campus: How a teaching center can make a difference.* Sterling, VA: Stylus.

Corcoran, M., & Clark, S. M. (1985). The stuck professor: Insights into an aspect of the faculty vitality issue. In C. Watson (Ed.), *The professoriate: Occupation in crisis* (pp. 57–81). Toronto, ON: Ontario Institute for Studies on Education.

Costantino, P. M., De Lorenzo, M. N., & Kobrinski, E. J. (2002). *Developing a professional teaching portfolio: A guide for success.* Boston, MA: Allyn & Bacon.

Covey, S. R. (2004). *The 7 habits of highly effective people.* London, UK: Simon & Schuster.

Cox, B. S., Cox, A. B., & Cox, D. J. (2000). Motivating signage prompts safety belt use among drivers exiting senior communities. *Journal of Applied Behavior Analysis, 33,* 635–638.

Cross, R. L., Cross, R. L., & Parker, A. (2004). *The hidden power of social networks: Understanding how work really gets done in organizations.* Cambridge, MA: Harvard Business Press.

Cross, R., Liedtka, J., & Weiss, L. (2005). A practical guide to social networks. *Harvard Business Review, 83*(3), 124–132.

Crow, R., Cruz, L., Ellern, J., Ford, G., Moss, H., & White, B. J. (2018). Boyer in the middle: Second generation challenges to emerging scholarship. *Innovative Higher Education, 43*(2), 107–123.

Cruz, L. (2017a). *Becoming a scholar of educational development.* Presentation given to the POD Network's Institute for New Faculty Developers, Saratoga Springs, NY.

Cruz, L. (2017b, November 10). *Scholar-practitioner: Transforming what you do into scholarship.* Presentation (virtual) given to POD Live! Series. Retrieved from https://podnetwork.org/event/podlive-scholar-practitioner-transforming-what-you-do-into-scholarship/

Cruz, L. (2018). The idea of educational development: An historical perspective. *To Improve the Academy, 37*(1), 159–171.

Cruz, L., Cunningham, K., Smentkowski, B., & Steiner, H. (2018). The SoTL scaffold: Supporting evidence-based teaching practice in educational development. *To Improve the Academy, 38*(1), 50–66.

Cruz, L., Jester-Huxtable, K., Smentkowski, B., & Springborg, M. (forthcoming). Place-based educational development: What center for teaching and learning spaces look like (and why that matters). *To Improve the Academy.* Retrieved from https://podnetwork.org/publications/to-improve-the-academy/

Cruz, L., & Reder, M. (2015). *Becoming a scholar of educational development.* Presentation given to the POD Network's Institute for New Faculty Developers, Asheville, NC.

Cruz, L. & Rosemond, L. (2017). Coaching academia: An integrated model of coaching and leadership in higher education, *Journal of Excellence in College Teaching, 28*(4), 83–108.

D'Avanzo, C. (2009). Supporting faculty through a new teaching and learning center. *Peer Review, 11*(2), 22–25.

Dawson, D., Britnell, J., & Hitchcock, A. (2010). Developing competency models of faculty developers: Using world café to foster dialogue. *To Improve the Academy, 28*, 3–24.

de Grave, W., Zanting, A., Mansvelder-Longayroux, D. D., Molenaar, W. M. (2014). Workshops and seminars: Enhancing effectiveness. In Y. Steinert (Ed.)., *Faculty Development in the Health Professions,* (pp. 181–195). Dordrecht, NL: Springer.

Diamond, R. M. (2005). The institutional change agency: The expanding role of academic support centers. *To Improve the Academy, 23,* 24–37.

Donnelli-Sallee, E., Dailey-Hebert, A., & Mandernach, B. J. (2012). Professional development for geographically dispersed faculty: Emerging trends, organizational challenges, and considerations for the future. *To Improve the Academy, 31*(1), 3–19.

Donnelly, R. (2007). Perceived impact of peer observation of teaching in higher education. *International Journal of Teaching and Learning in Higher Education, 19*(2), 117–129.

Drake, E., Bowdon, M., & Saitta, E. (2012, October 27). *Planning for success: Strategic planning and faculty development center advocacy.* Presentation given to the POD Network Annual Conference, Seattle, WA.

Eisend, M. (2007). Understanding two-sided persuasion: An empirical assessment of theoretical approaches. *Psychology and Marketing, 24,* 615–640.

Elliott, M., Rhoades, N., Jackson, C. M., & Mandernach, J. B. (2015). Professional development: Designing initiatives to meet the needs of online faculty. *Journal of Educators Online, 12*(1), 160–188.

Felten, P., Kalish, A., Pingree, A., & Plank, K. (2007). Toward a scholarship of teaching and learning in educational development. In D. Robertson & L. Nilson (Eds.), *To improve the academy: Resources for faculty, instructional and organizational development,* Vol. 25 (pp. 93–108). San Francisco, CA: Jossey-Bass.

Felten, P., Little, D., & Pingree, A. (2004). Foucault and the practice of educational development: Power and surveillance in individual consultations. In C. Wehlburg & S. Chadwick-Blossey (Eds.), *To improve the academy: Resources for faculty, instructional and organizational development*, Vol. 21 (pp. 173–188). San Francisco, Jossey-Bass.

Fernández-Huerga, E. (2008). The economic behavior of human beings: The institutional/post-Keynesian model. *Journal of Economic Issues, 42*(3), 709–726.

Finelli, C. J., Ott, M., Gottfried, A. C., Hershock, C., O'Neal, C., & Kaplan, M. (2008). Utilizing instructional consultations to enhance the teaching performance of engineering faculty. *Journal of Engineering Education, 97*(4), 397–411.

Freeman, S., Eddy, S. L., McDonough, M., Smith, M. K., Okoroafor, N., Jordt, H., & Wenderoth, M. P. (2014). Active learning increases student performance in science, engineering, and mathematics. *Proceedings of the National Academy of Sciences, 111*(23), 8410–8415.

Friedel, J. N., & Rosenberg, D. (1993). Environmental scanning practices in junior, technical, and community colleges. *Community College Review, 20*(5), 16–22.

Fry, J. P., & Neff, R. A. (2009). Periodic prompts and reminders in health promotion and health behavior interventions: Systematic review. *Journal of Medical Internet Research, 11*(2), e16.

Fugate, A. L., & Amey, M. J. (2000). Career stages of community college faculty: A qualitative analysis of their career paths, roles, and development. *Community College Review, 28*(1), 1–22.

Fugazzotto, S. J. (2009). Mission statements, physical space, and strategy in higher education. *Innovative Higher Education, 34*(5), 285–298.

Gappa, J. M., Austin, A. E., & Trice, A. G. (2007). *Rethinking faculty work: Higher education's strategic imperative*. San Francisco, CA: Jossey-Bass.

Gardner, S. K. (2005). Faculty preparation for teaching, research, and service roles: What do new faculty need? *Journal of Faculty Development, 20*(3), 161–166.

Gibbs, G. (2013). Reflections on the changing nature of educational development. *International Journal for Academic Development, 18*(1), 4–14.

Gibbs, G., & Coffey, M. (2004). The impact of training of university teachers on their teaching skills, their approach to teaching and the approach to learning of their students. *Active Learning in Higher Education, 5*(1), 87–100.

Gladwell, M. (2006). *The tipping point: How little things can make a big difference*. New York, NY: Little Brown.

Godert, A., & Kenyon, K. (2013, November 8). *Counting connections: Learning, communicating, and reporting with a database*. Session presented at the 38th Annual POD Conference, Pittsburgh, Pennsylvania.

Goetsch, D. L., & Davis, S. B. (2014). *Quality management for organizational excellence*. Upper Saddle River, NJ: Pearson.

Gollwitzer, P. M., & Sheeran, P. (2006). Implementation intentions and goal achievement: A meta-analysis of effects and processes. In M. P. Zanna (Ed.), *Advances in experimental social psychology* (Vol. 38, pp. 69–120). San Diego, CA: Elsevier.

Grant, B., Lee, A., Clegg, S., Manathunga, C., Barrow, M., Kandlbinder, P., Brailsford, I., Gosling, D. & Hicks, M. (2009). Why history? Why now? Multiple accounts of the emergence of academic development. *International Journal for Academic Development, 14*(1), 83–86.

Grant-Vallone, E. J., & Ensher, E. A. (2017). Re-crafting careers for mid-career faculty: A qualitative study. *Journal of Higher Education Theory and Practice, 17*(5), 10–24.

Gravett, E. O., & Bernhagen, L. (2015). A view from the margins: Situating CTL staff in organizational development. *To Improve the Academy, 34*(1-2), 63–90.

Gray, T., & Shadle, S. (2009). Launching or revitalizing a teaching center: Principles and portraits of practice. *Journal of Faculty Development, 23*(2), 5–12.

Green, D. A., & Little, D. (2013). Academic development on the margins. *Studies in Higher Education, 38*(4), 523–537.

Green, D. A., & Little, D. (2016). Family portrait: A profile of educational developers around the world. *International Journal for Academic Development, 21*(2), 135–150.

Green, D. A., & Little, D. (2017). On the other side of the wall: The miscategorization of educational developers in the United States? *To Improve the Academy, 36*(2), 77–88.

Greenwald, H.P., & Zukoski, A.P. (2018). Assessing collaboration: Alternative measures and issues for evaluation. *American Journal of Evaluation, 39*(3), 322–335.

Hagen, K. M., Gutkin, T. B., Wilson, C. P., & Oats, R. G. (1998). Using vicarious experience and verbal persuasion to enhance self-efficacy in pre-service teachers: "Priming the pump" for consultation. *School Psychology Quarterly, 13*(2), 169–178.

Hagger, M. S., & Luszczynska, A. (2014). Implementation intention and action planning interventions in health contexts: State of the research and proposals for the way forward. *Applied Psychology: Health and Well-Being, 6*(1), 1–47.

Haras, C., Ginsberg, M., Magruder, E. D., & Zakrajsek, T. (2019*). A beta faculty development center matrix.* Washington, DC: American Council on Education. Retrieved from http://www.acenet.edu/news-room/Documents/A-Beta-Faculty-Development-Center-Matrix.pdf

Haras, C., Taylor, S. C., Sorcinelli, M. D., & van Hoene, L. (2017). *Institutional commitment to teaching excellence: Assessing the impacts and outcomes of faculty development.* Washington, DC: American Council on Education.

Harland, T., & Staniforth, D. (2003). Academic development as academic work. *International Journal for Academic Development, 8*(1–2), 25–35.

Harland, T., & Staniforth, D. (2008). A family of strangers: The fragmented nature of academic development. *Teaching in Higher Education, 13*(6), 669–678.

Hax, A. C., & Majluf, N. S. (1996). *The strategy concept and process: A pragmatic approach* (2nd ed., pp. 360–375). Upper Saddle River, NJ: Prentice Hall.

Head, K. J., & Noar, S. M. (2014). Facilitating progress in health behaviour theory development and modification: The reasoned action approach as a case study. *Health Psychology Review, 8*(1), 34–52.

Henderson, C., Beach, A., & Finkelstein, N. (2011). Facilitating change in undergraduate STEM instructional practices: An analytic review of the literature. *Journal of Research in Science Teaching, 48*(8), 952–984.

Hendricks, C. (2015, November 9–13). *Taking flight*: Needs assessment. Presentation at the POD Network Annual Conference, San Francisco, CA.

Herckis, L. (2018). Cultivating practice: Ensuring continuity, acknowledging change. *Practicing Anthropology, 40*(1), 43–47.

Hines, S. R. (2009a). *Creating and assessing faculty development programs.* Retrieved from https://sites.google.com/a/podnetwork.org/wikipodia/Home/topics-for-discussion/assessing-faculty-development-programs

Hines, S. R. (2009b). Investigating faculty development program assessment practices: What's being done and how can it be improved? *Journal of Faculty Development, 23*(3), 5–19.

Hines, S. R. (2011). How mature teaching and learning centers evaluate their services. *To Improve the Academy, 30*(1), 277–289.

Hines, S. R. (2015). Setting the groundwork for quality faculty development evaluation: A five-step approach. *The Journal of Faculty Development, 29*(1), 5–12.

Hines, S. R. (2017). Evaluating centers for teaching and learning: A field-tested model. *To Improve the Academy, 36*(2), 89–100.

hooks, b. (1990). *Yearnings: Race, gender, and cultural politics.* Boston, MA: South Press.

Hurney, C. A., Brantmeier, E. J., Good, M. R., Harrison, D., & Meizner, C. (2016). The faculty learning outcome assessment framework. *Journal of Faculty Development, 30*(2), 69–77.

Huston, T. A., Norman, M., & Ambrose, S. A. (2007). Expanding the discussion of faculty vitality to include productive but disengaged senior faculty. *Journal of Higher Education, 78*(5), 493–522.

Huston, T., & Weaver, C. L. (2008). Peer coaching: Professional development for experienced faculty. *Innovative Higher Education, 33*(1), 5–20.

Hutchings, P. (2007). Theory: The elephant in the scholarship of teaching and learning room. *International Journal for the Scholarship of Teaching and Learning, 1*(1), 2.

Introduction to Assessing Community Needs. (2013). *Strengthening extension advisory leaders.* Retrieved from https://campus.extension.org/mod/page/view.php?id=26519

Johnson, W. B. (2015). *On being a mentor: A guide for higher education faculty.* New York, NY: Routledge.

Jung, T., Scott, T., Davies, H. T., Bower, P., Whalley, D., McNally, R., & Mannion, R. (2009). Instruments for exploring organizational culture: A review of the literature. *Public Administration Review, 69*(6), 1087–1096.

Kahn, P. (2004). Careers within staff and educational development. In D. Baume & P. Kahn (Eds.), *Enhancing staff and educational development* (pp. 174–189). New York, NY: Routledge.

Kalivoda, P., Sorrell, G. R., & Simpson, R. D. (1994, June). Nurturing faculty vitality by matching institutional interventions with career-stage needs. *Innovative Higher Education, 18*, 255–272.

Kelley, B. (2018). Good to great in educational development. *To Improve the Academy, 37*(1), 151–158.

Kelley, B., Cruz, L., & Fire, N. (2017). Moving toward the center: The integration of educational development in an era of historic change in higher education. *To Improve the Academy, 36*(1), 1–8.

Kezar, A. (2001). Understanding and facilitating organizational change in the 21st century: Recent research and conceptualizations. *ASHE-ERIC Higher Education Report, 28*(4). San Francisco, CA: Jossey-Bass. Retrieved from https://eric.ed.gov/?id=ED457711

Kezar, A. (2014). Higher education change and social networks: A review of research. *The Journal of Higher Education, 85*(1), 91–125.

Kezar, A., & Eckel, P. D. (2002). The effect of institutional culture on change strategies in higher education: Universal principles or culturally responsive concepts? *The Journal of Higher Education, 73*(4), 435–460.

Kolomitro, K., & Anstey, L. M. (2017). A survey on evaluation practices in teaching and learning centres. *International Journal for Academic Development, 22*(3), 186–198.

Knight, P. T. (2002). *Small-scale research. Pragmatic inquiry in social science and the caring professions.* London, UK: SAGE.

Kowalik, A., Bostwick Faming, A. A., Fulmer, S. M., Donnell, A. M., & Smith, T. W. (2016, November 10). *Developing the developers: Growing transformative relationships through a mentoring network.* Presentation given at the POD Network Conference, Louisville, KY.

Kreber, C., & Brook, P. (2001). Impact evaluation of educational development programmes. *International Journal for Academic Development, 6*(2), 96–108.

Land, R. (2001). Agency, context and change in academic development. *International Journal for Academic Development, 6*(1), 4–20.

Lang, J. M. (2016). *Small teaching: Everyday lessons from the science of learning.* San Francisco, CA: Wiley.

Lee, A., & McWilliam, E. (2008). What game are we in? Living with academic development. *International Journal for Academic Development, 13*(1), 67–77.

Leibowitz, B. (2014). Reflections on academic development: What is in a name? *International Journal for Academic Development, 19*(4), 357–360.

Lewis, K. G. (1996). Faculty development in the United States: A brief history. *The International Journal for Academic Development, 1*(2), 26–33.

Lewis, K. G., & Kristensen, E. (1997). A global faculty development network: The International Consortium for Educational Development (ICED). *To Improve the Academy, 16*(1), 53–66.

Liebowitz, J. (2007). *Social networking: The essence of innovation*. Lanham, MD: Scarecrow Press.

Lieff, S. J. (2009). Perspective: The missing link in academic career planning and development: Pursuit of meaningful and aligned work. *Academic Medicine, 84*(10), 1383–1388.

Linse, A. (2018, June 5–8). *Using strategic planning to evaluate academic development units*. Presentation given to the International Consortium for Educational Development conference, Atlanta, GA.

Little, D. (2014). Reflections on the state of the scholarship of educational development. *To Improve the Academy, 33*(1), 1–13.

Little, D., & Green, D. A. (2012). Betwixt and between: Academic developers in the margins. *International Journal for Academic Development, 17*(3), 203–215.

Little, D., & Palmer, M. (2011). A coaching-based framework for individual consultations. In J. Miller & J. Groccia (Eds.), *To Improve the Academy: Resources for Faculty, Instructional and Organizational Development, 29*, 102–115.

Lohe, D. (2012, October 24–28). *Illuminating "lived experiences": Strategic planning in teaching and learning centers (TLCs)*. Presentation to the POD Network Annual Conference, Seattle, WA.

Macfadyen, L. P., Groth, D., Rehrey, G., Shepard, L., Greer, J., Ward, D., & Steinwachs, M. (2017, March). Developing institutional learning analytics' communities of transformation' to support student success. In *Proceedings of the Seventh International Learning Analytics & Knowledge Conference* (pp. 498–499). ACM.

Manathunga, C. (2006). Doing educational development ambivalently: Applying post-colonial metaphors to educational development? *International Journal for Academic Development, 11*(1), 19–29.

Matthews, K. R. (2014). Perspectives on mid-career faculty and advice for supporting them. *Collaborative on Academic Careers in Higher Education (COACHE) Report*. Retrieved from www.coache.org

Maxwell, W. E., & Kazlauskas, E. J. (1992). Which faculty development methods really work in community colleges? A review of research. *Community/Junior College Quarterly of Research and Practice, 16*(4), 351–360.

McCaffery, P. (2018). *The higher education manager's handbook: Effective leadership and management in universities and colleges* (3rd ed.). New York, NY: Routledge.

McDonald, J., & Stockley, D. (2008). Pathways to the profession of educational development: An international perspective. *International Journal for Academic Development, 13*(3), 213–218.

McDonald, J., Kenny, N., Kustra, E., Dawson, D., Iqbal, I., Borin, P., & Chan, J. (2016). *Educational development guide series: No. 1. The educational developer's portfolio*. Ottawa, Canada: Educational Developers Caucus.

McKendree, A. (2012, October 24–28). *Integrated marketing communications: In with the old in with the new*. Presentation given to the POD Network annual conference, Seattle, WA.

Meixell, J. (1990, July 30). *Environmental scanning activities at public research and doctorate-granting universities.* Paper presented at a meeting of the Society for College and University Planning, Atlanta, GA.

Meyer, L. H., & Evans, I. M. (2005). Supporting academic staff: Meeting new expectations in higher education without compromising traditional faculty values. *Higher Education Policy, 18*(3), 243–255.

Milloy, P., & Brooke, C. (2004). Beyond bean counting: Making faculty development needs assessment more meaningful. *To Improve the Academy, 22*(1), 71–92.

Mooney, K. M., & Reder, M. (2008). 11: Faculty development at small and liberal arts colleges. *To Improve the Academy, 26*(1), 158–172.

Murray, J. P. (2002). The current state of faculty development in two-year colleges. *New Directions for Community Colleges, 118,* 89–98.

Nadler, M. K., Shore, C., Taylor, B. A. P., & Bakker, A. I. (2012). *Making waves:* Demonstrating a CTL's impact on teaching and learning. *Journal on Centers for Teaching and Learning, 4,* 5–32.

Naliaka Mukhale, P. (2017, January 1). Towards improvement of student learning outcomes: An assessment of the professional development needs of lecturers at Kenyan universities. *Journal of Education and Practice 8*(12), 151–158.

Narayanan, V. K., & Fahey, L. (2001). Macroenvironmental analysis: Understanding the environment outside the industry. In L. Fahey & R. M. Randall (Eds.), *The portable MBA in strategy* (pp. 189–214). New York, NY: John Wiley & Sons.

Ng, W. (Ed.). (2015). Adopting new digital technologies in education: Professional learning. In *New digital technology in education: Conceptualizing professional learning for educators* (pp. 25–48). Basel, Switzerland: Springer.

O'Keefe, D. J. (2016). *Persuasion: Theory and research* (3rd ed.). Thousand Oaks, CA: SAGE.

O'Meara, K. A., Terosky, A. L., & Neumann, A. (2008). Faculty careers and work lives: A professional growth perspective. *ASHE Higher Education Report, 4*(3), 1–221.

Ortquist-Ahrens, L. (2016). Beyond survival: Educational development and the maturing of the POD Network. *To Improve the Academy, 35*(1), 1–34.

Osita, C., Idoko, O., & Justina, N. (2014). Organization's stability and productivity: The role of SWOT analysis. *International Journal of Innovative and Applied Resources, 2*(9), 23–32.

Ouellett, M. L. (2010). Overview of faculty development. In K. J. Gillespie, D. L. Robertson & Associates (Eds.), *A guide to faculty development* (2nd ed., pp. 3–20). San Francisco, CA: Jossey-Bass.

Parkman, A. (2016). The imposter phenomenon in higher education: Incidence and impact. *Journal of Higher Education Theory and Practice, 16*(1), 51–60.

Pastore, D. L. (2013). Faculty perspectives on Baldwin and Chang's mid-career faculty development model. *Journal of Faculty Development, 27*(2), 25–32.

Patton, M. Q. (2008). *Utilization-focused evaluation.* Thousand Oaks, CA: SAGE.

Peresellin, D., & Goodrick, T. (2010). Faculty development in higher education: Long-term impact of a summer teaching and learning workshop. *Journal of the Scholarship of Teaching and Learning, 10*(1), 1–13.

Pettit, T., & Kenyon, K. (2012, October 24–28). *If you build it, will they come? Marketing your center*. Presentation given to the POD Network annual conference, Seattle, WA.

Plank, K., & Kalish, A. (2010). Program assessment for faculty development. In K. J. Gillespie & D. L. Robertson, (Eds.), *A guide to faculty development*. (2nd ed., pp. 135–149). San Francisco, CA: Jossey-Bass.

Plank, K. M., Kalish, A., Rohdieck, S. V., & Harper, K. A. (2005). A vision beyond measurement: Creating an integrated data system for teaching centers. In S. Chadwick-Blossey & D. R. Robertson (Eds.), *To Improve the Academy, 23,* 173–190.

POD Network. (n.d.). *Ethical guidelines*. Retrieved from https://podnetwork.org/about-us/pod-governance/ethical-guidelines/

Poole, G. D. (2007). Using the scholarship of teaching and learning at disciplinary, national and institutional levels to strategically improve the quality of post-secondary education. *International Journal for the Scholarship of Teaching and Learning, 1*(2), 3.

Reder, M. (2007). Does your college really support teaching and learning? *Peer Review, 9*(4). Retrieved from https://www.aacu.org/publications-research/periodicals/does-your-college-really-support-teaching-and-learning

Roberts, J. (2018). Future and changing roles of staff in distance education: A study to identify training and professional development needs. *Distance Education, 39*(1), 37–53.

Robertson, D. (2010). Establishing an educational development program. In K. J. Gillespie, D. L. Robertson (Eds.), *A guide to faculty development* (2nd ed., pp. 35–52). San Francisco, CA: Wiley.

Robison, S. (2013). *The peak performing professor: A practical guide to productivity and happiness*. San Francisco, CA: Wiley.

Rowley, D. J. (1997). *Strategic change in colleges and universities: Planning to survive and prosper*. San Francisco, CA: Jossey-Bass.

Roxå, T., & Martensson, K. (2009). Significant conversations and significant networks—exploring the backstage of the teaching arena. *Studies in Higher Education, 34,* 547–559.

Ruben, B. D. (2005). *Excellence in higher education: An integrated approach to assessment, planning, and improvement in colleges and universities*. Washington, DC: National Association of College and University Business Officers.

Rudenga, K. J., & Gravett, E. O. (2019). Impostor phenomenon in educational developers. *To Improve the Academy, 38*(1), 1–17.

Schmieder-Ramirez, J., & Mallette, L. (2015). Using the SPELIT analysis technique for organizational transitions. In M. Carmo (Ed.), *Education applications & Developments Advances in Education and Educational Trends Series* (pp. 290–302). Retrieved from http://insciencepress.org/wp-content/uploads/2015/05/ISP_Education-Applications-Developments-Book.pdf

Schön, D. A. (2017). *The reflective practitioner: How professionals think in action.* New York, NY: Routledge.

Schroeder, C. (2012). *Coming in from the margins: Faculty development's emerging organizational development role in institutional change.* Sterling, VA: Stylus.

Schroeder, C. (2015). Unpacking and communicating the multidimensional mission of educational development: A mission matrix tool for centers of teaching and learning. *To Improve the Academy, 34*(1), 20–62.

Scott, T., Mannion, R., Davies, H., & Marshall, M. (2003). The quantitative measurement of organizational culture in health care: A review of the available instruments. *Health Services Research, 38*(3), 923–945.

Seldin, P., Miller, J. E., & Seldin, C. A. (2010). *The teaching portfolio: A practical guide to improved performance and promotion/tenure decisions.* San Francisco, CA: Wiley.

Shahid, A. (2012). Faculty perspective of faculty development. *Academic Leader, 28*(7), 2.

Shaker, G. G., & Palmer, M. M. (2012). The donors next door: Raising funds from faculty for faculty development centers. *To Improve the Academy, 31*(1), 85–99.

Shinnar, R. S., & Williams, H. L. (2008). Promoting faculty diversity: The faculty fellows program at Appalachian State University. *Planning for Higher Education, 36*(2), 42–53.

Shulman, L. S. (2007). Counting and recounting: Assessment and the quest for accountability. *Change, 39*(1), 20–25.

Siering, G. J., Tapp, S., Lohe, D. R., & Logan, M. M. (2015). Negotiating a seat at the table: Questions to guide institutional involvement. *To Improve the Academy, 34*(1), 171–193.

Sorcinelli, M. D. (2002). Ten principles of good practices in creating and sustaining teaching and learning centers. In K. Gillespie (Ed.), *A guide to faculty development: Practical advice, examples, and resources* (pp. 9–23). San Francisco, CA: Jossey-Bass.

Sorcinelli, M. D., Austin, A. E., & Eddy, P. L. (2006). *Creating the future of faculty development: Learning from the past, understanding the present* (Vol. 59). San Francisco, CA: Jossey-Bass.

Springborg, M., & Horri, C. (2016). Toward a new creative scholarship of educational development: The teaching and learning project and an opening to discourse. *To Improve the Academy: A Journal of Educational Development, 35*(2), 197–221.

Stark, A. M., & Smith, G. A. (2016). Communities of practice as agents of future faculty development. *The Journal of Faculty Development, 30*(2), 59–67.

Sutherland, K. A., & Hill, M. (2018). The 'impact' of academic development. *International Journal for Academic Development, 23*(2), 69–71.

Sweet, C., & Blythe, H. (2010). Integrating CTLs into campus strategic planning through an effective brainstorming process. *Journal on Centers for Teaching and Learning, 2,* 71–89.

Sweet, M., Roberts, R., Walker, J., Walls, S., Kucsera, J., Shaw, S., & Svinicki, M. (2008). 6: Grounded theory research in faculty development: The basics, a live example, and practical tips for faculty developers. *To Improve the Academy, 26*(1), 89–105.

Taylor, K. L., Colet, N. R., Saroyan, A., & Frenay, M. (2012). Making the shift from faculty development to educational development. In A. Saroyan & M. Frenay (Eds.), *Building teaching capacities in higher education: A comprehensive international model* (pp. 139–167). Sterling, VA: Stylus.

Temple, P. (Ed.). (2014). *The physical university: Contours of space and place in higher education*. New York, NY: Routledge.

Timmermans, J. A. (2014). Identifying threshold concepts in the careers of educational developers. *International Journal for Academic Development, 19*(4), 305–317.

Verboncu, I. & Condurache, A. (2016). Diagnostics vs. SWOT analysis. *Revista de Management Comparat International, 17*(2), 114–122.

Weimer, M. (2007). Intriguing connections but not with the past. *International Journal for Academic Development, 12*(1), 5–8.

Weinstein, S., Linse, A., & Brua, C. (2011, October 26–30). *Improving impact and enhancing accountability: Strategic planning for teaching centers*. Presentation given to the POD Network annual conference, Atlanta, GA.

Wergin, J. F. (2001). Beyond carrots and sticks: What really motivates faculty. *Liberal Education, 87*(1), 50–53.

Wiggins, G. P., Wiggins, G., & McTighe, J. (2005). *Understanding by design*. Alexandria, VA: Association for Supervision and Curriculum Development.

Williams, A. L., Verwoord, R., Beery, T. A., Dalton, H., McKinnon, J., Strickland, K., Pace, J. & Poole, G. (2013). The power of social networks: A model for weaving the scholarship of teaching and learning into institutional culture. *Teaching and Learning Inquiry: The ISSOTL Journal, 1*(2), 49–62.

Winter, R. (2009). Academic manager or managed academic? Academic identity schisms in higher education. *Journal of Higher Education Policy and Management, 31*(2), 121–131.

Wright, D. L. (2002). Program types and prototypes. In K. H. Gillespie, L. R. Hilsen, & E. C. Wadsworth (Eds.), *A guide to faculty development: Practical advice, examples, and resources* (pp. 24–34). Bolton, MA: Anker.

Wright, M., Horii, C.V., Felten, P., Sorcinelli, M.D., & Kaplan, M. (2018). Faculty development improves teaching and learning. *POD Speaks 2*, 1–5. Retrieved from https://podnetwork.org/content/uploads/POD-Speaks-Issue-2_Jan2018-1.pdf

Wright, M. C. (2011). Measuring a teaching center's effectiveness. In C. E. Cook & M. Kaplan (Eds.), *Advancing the culture of teaching on campus: How a teaching center can make a difference* (pp. 38-49). Sterling, VA: Stylus.

Wright, M.C., Cook, C.E., & Brady, E. (2000). Using grants to enhance student learning. *CRLT Occasional Paper, 13*, 9–23. Retrieved from http://www.crlt.umich.edu/sites/default/files/resource_files/CRLT_no13.pdf

Wright, M. C., Lohe, D. R., Pinder-Grover, T., & Ortquist-Ahrens, L. (2018). The four Rs: Guiding CTLs with responsiveness, relationships, resources, and research. *To Improve the Academy, 37*(2), 271–286.

Wright, W. A., & Miller, J. (2000). The educational developer's portfolio. *International Journal for Academic Development, 5*(1), 20–29. Retrieved from http://www .tandfonline.com/doi/abs/10.1080/136014400410079#.UgUrG6y0RI0

Zakrajsek, T. D. (2010). Important skills and knowledge. In K. J. Gillespie & D. L. Robertson (Eds.), A guide to faculty development (2nd ed.). San Francisco, CA: Jossey-Bass.

Zeig, M. J. & Baldwin, R. G. (2013). Keeping the fire burning: Strategies to support senior faculty. In J. Groccia & L. Cruz (Eds.), *To improve the academy: Resources for faculty, instructional and organizational development* (Vol. 32, pp. 73–88). San Francisco, CA: Jossey-Bass.

ABOUT THE AUTHORS

Laura Cruz (Ph.D., UC Berkeley 2001) is an Associate Research Professor for Teaching & Learning Scholarship with the Schreyer Institute for Teaching Excellence at Penn State. She previously served as the director of two Centers for Teaching and Learning; as editor-in-chief of three teaching-related journals, as elected member of the national board for faculty developers in the United States, and as principle investigator for four externally funded grants. Her publications and invited presentations include work in her first discipline (history)  as well as the areas of instructional design, educational development, the scholarship of teaching and learning, organizational change, and educational innovation.

Michele Parker is from Brooklyn, NY. She was a non-traditional college student at SUNY Stonybrook. Encouraged by the excellent mentoring received in college, Parker pursued a Master's degree in Higher Education and Student Affairs Administration. Later she earned a Ph.D. in Research, Statistics, and Evaluation at the University of Virginia and then joined the faculty at UNC Wilmington (UNCW). In the Educational Leadership department, Parker teaches inquiry courses. Also, she teaches for the college teaching certificate and the coach-ing and mentoring certificate programs. At the University, she serves on University-wide Task Forces. In educational development, Parker previously worked in a Center for Teaching and Learning. Currently, she leads faculty development initiatives transnationally.

Brian Smentkowski is the Founding Director of the Center for Excellence in Teaching and Learning, Director of Service Learning, and Associate Professor of Political Science at the University of Idaho. He is the past editor of *To Improve the Academy: A Journal of Educational Development* and has published and presented extensively in the fields of educational development and political science. He has led faculty and educational development programs and initiatives at four universities, with an emphasis on institutional culture change, SoTL, and supporting student success through faculty and educational development.

Marina Smitherman is Chair of the Department of Life Sciences and Professor of Biology at Dalton State College. With two decades of college teaching experience, Smitherman has specialized in Educational and Organizational Development; serving as Director of the Center for Academic Excellence leading faculty development in Teaching and Learning, leading High Impact Practice curriculum innovations, chairing the Georgia Consortium of Teaching and Learning Directors, and working collaborative on scholarship with POD, CUR, and AAC&U colleagues. She won the University System of Georgia Felton Jenkins Jr. Faculty Hall of Fame Teaching Excellence Award in 2020.